RED
BRAIN
BLUE
BRAIN

RED BRAIN BLUE BRAIN

LIVING LOVING LEADING WITHOUT FEAR

JOHN CORRIGAN

First paperback edition published 2019
46 Tebbutt Street
Leichhardt NSW 2040

Cover design by Pulp Studio
Layout by Lu Sexton

Corrigan, John.

Red Brain Blue Brain.

ISBN 978-0-9946044-2-2 pbk, 978-0-9946044-3-9 ebk

'You mad millenial bastard' by Frank Robson reprinted with permission.

To my wife, Maryse,
and my children – Lina Maria, Laura and
Duncan – for whom all this is worth it.

ABOUT THE AUTHOR

John works with schools to help them achieve the conditions for twenty-first-century learning. He helps individuals bring their whole of mind to their daily lives, increasing their own effectiveness and that of those around them. This is his passion.

Born in Manchester, England, he moved to Australia in 1995 but the journey to this point roved through nine countries, where he picked up four languages, and ranged through a number of careers. He was an officer in the Parachute Regiment and a wireline logging engineer in South America (taking measurements in drilled oil and gas wells), before entering the corporate sector via strategy consulting and corporate planning.

John has had a strong interest in education since 2001 and set up Group 8 Education in 2003 to help in the transformation of our education systems.

Now living in Melbourne, when not training, coaching or writing, John enjoys travel, Australian rules football, good cinema and good food.

John is the author of three other books:

- *A World Fit for Children* (2005)
- *The Success Zone* (2009) with Andrew Mowat and Doug Long
- *Optimising Time, Attention and Energy (2016)*

CONTENTS

PREFACE

A transformation is taking place in our education systems. We see a great deal of effort going into curriculum and pedagogy; however my particular interest lies in the relationship between educator and student – an aspect of education that is less well resourced, though no less important.

Over the past seventeen years, I have come to understand how important this relationship is for our children's healthy development; further, that it still reflects the priorities and beliefs of earlier times, therefore limiting the growth that we need for the twenty-first century, rather than supporting and catalysing it.

We are social creatures and we grow healthily in deep connection with others. Indeed, as I argue in this book, strong healthy relationships with others – even those from whom we are different – are critical for success in work and life in the twenty-first century. However, in today's societies, unhealthy relationships predominate (transactional, coercive, controlling, dependent, needy). The teaching profession can lead the way in modelling deep connection with others.

In functional terms, the relationship between educator and child has been, and continues to be, on a long journey. The starting point, enshrined in state schooling systems when they were first put in place two centuries ago, is where the educator provided summative feedback – pass/fail, grades or marks – and was not interested in what the child had to say; after all, the teacher knew best.

We are heading towards a space where the educator provides formative feedback to the child, and the child provides formative feedback in return. Both grow, and more quickly, because they are able to accept and use the feedback they receive. The starting point was a one-sided, controlling relationship designed to transmit knowledge. The point towards which we are heading is a mutual, respectful and trusting relationship: co-creating learning.

Today we recognise that relationships are important for effective education, but lack clarity as to what an effective educator–student relationship looks like, and how to achieve it. Likewise, we recognise that providing formative feedback to the child is more valuable than summative feedback. Less well recognised is the value of student feedback back to the educator; although this also is growing in acceptance.

We can develop this critical educator–child relationship in three ways:

1. Provide systematic student feedback to educators to stimulate individual and whole-school changes in practice, and prepare the way for formative feedback from students.

2. Help educators so that they can respond to student feedback (however it might be given) without feeling affronted or frustrated; but, rather, respond in a way that puts the student in the ideal frame of mind for learning.

3. Help school leaders to model to teachers the same type of relationship – of mutuality, trust and deep respect – that teachers need to develop with their students.

This book, one of three, is focused on the second of these areas. Books focusing on the first and third areas are scheduled for publication in 2019 and 2020, respectively.

Introduction

Have you ever found yourself unable to speak coherently in an interview, been disarmed by your sudden rage at something minor, or noticed that – *typical* – all the other supermarket queues are moving faster than yours?

This is your red brain triggering.

Most humans experience life through two brain states. In our blue brain, we are at our best – confident, collaborative and creative; in our red brain, negative feelings emerge; our focus narrows; and we ruminate over past events, indulging in negative self-talk. In the red brain we are not at all at our best.

Having two brains is not a natural condition for humans, and the existence of the red brain limits us in so many ways. At one extreme, the red brain is responsible for the uncontrolled violence that is present in road rage; at the other extreme is the complete withdrawal and apathy associated with chronic depression. When the red brain is active we have very limited control over ourselves; we lack choice in our responses, which are therefore automatic; and our ability to learn is reduced, essentially, to simple, repetitive tasks.

The two-brain state seems normal because it is all most of us have ever known. It has been developed and reinforced over centuries, flourishing alongside the hierarchical organisation of society that has enabled humankind to survive and create the world we see around us today.

Ever since humans first settled down into agriculture, which is characterised by algorithmic (easily sequenced) routines, rewards and punishments have been used to get us to work harder and longer than we might choose to on our own. Although some of the work has been to provide for our needs, a good proportion has been appropriated by a small elite to provide themselves with a comfortable life.

In his best-selling book, *Sapiens: a brief history of humankind*, author Yuval Noah Harari argues that:

> Hunter-gatherers spent their time in more stimulating and varied ways, and were less in danger of starvation and disease. The Agricultural Revolution certainly enlarged the sum total of food at the disposal of humankind, but the extra food did not translate into a better diet or more leisure. Rather, it translated into population explosions and pampered elites. The average farmer worked harder than the average forager, and got a worse diet in return.

It is easy to imagine that, once there was a supply of food that would see a small village community through until the next harvest, it was worth stealing. Perhaps, at first, a more aggressive group might have stolen out of desperation for food; then subsequently realised that, rather than taking everything, they could take a proportion and offer their protection in return. The farmers would have had to work harder to support this additional "tax". Such an aggressive group could then have settled down and "taxed" a range of villages within their territory. To keep the villagers from rebelling, they would have needed to coerce and bully anyone who stood up to them.

As is explained in this book, controlling someone's motivation (in this case, through threat of punishment) distorts the process of becoming a self-directed, blue-brain adult: it fosters the development of a red brain.

Gradually, the aggressor group would have seen themselves as superior: their children would have developed normally as their hunter-gatherer ancestors had; whereas the peasants would have been fearful and cowed. And so the separation of the rulers and the ruled became the natural order of things.

But you cannot control things indefinitely with the threat of violence. Humans are unique in their ability to create fictions or stories that are believed and shared. Harari again:

> Telling effective stories is not easy. The difficulty lies not in telling the story, but in convincing everyone else to believe it. Much of history revolves around this question: how does one convince millions of people to believe particular stories about gods, or nations, or limited liability companies? Yet when it succeeds, it gives Sapiens immense power, because it enables millions of strangers to cooperate and work towards common goals. Just try to imagine how difficult it would have been to create states, or churches, or legal systems if we could speak only about things that really exist, such as rivers, trees and lions.

Gradually stories were developed and believed – developed not by the men of violence but by sorcerers and priests who supported them – that legitimised this new order. In Europe, a widespread and persistent belief was the divine right of kings: that kings must be obeyed because they had been appointed by God. Yet behind this story stood the threat of violence.

With such an arrangement in place, humankind has continued the same pattern; wars and revolutions have changed who's in charge, but not the underlying structure. This structure has led to the developed world that we live in today, but the dysfunctional elements peculiar to hierarchical arrangements have led us to the over-exploitation of both the human and natural worlds.

While controlled motivation has created the red brain, state compulsory education has more systematically reinforced the two-brain state over the last two hundred years. Modern societies accommodate this two-brain state, and further reinforce it through an economic model that relies on motivating the large majority to complete sequential work through reward and punishment.

Now, in the twenty-first century, we are at a unique moment in history where a sizeable proportion of this simple, repetitive work can be done by robots and computers. While fewer people will be employed doing work that can be automated, more people will be needed for complex work. Jobs for humans will demand us to be collaborative, creative and confident – in short: that we operate in the blue brain.

The two-brain state has become an impediment, crippling our ability to solve contemporary problems. Complex issues, some of which threaten our very existence, also demand a blue-brain approach – a creative and collaborative approach to problem solving.

To operate in the blue brain, we need to be motivated, not by reward or punishment (controlled motivation), but to do something because we are interested or we enjoy it; or, if it is neither enjoyable nor interesting, because it connects to a deeply held value that we have: we need to be autonomously motivated. Autonomous motivation avoids the creation of the red brain. Without a red brain people are not easily controlled; they have courage and can act in ways that seem right to them that may challenge the status quo.

The recognition that we now need to develop young people using autonomous motivation rather than trying to control their behaviour through controlled motivation is a profound shift.

This book will show how the two-brain state has developed, and been maintained in modern times, why it is no longer serving us, and what we can do to become our best – both as individuals and societies. We have a very real possibility of creating a blue brain world; a world that can face up to the existential problems of our age – climate change and resource depletion – with a real chance of being able to find solutions to these very complex problems. Unconstrained by a red brain, individuals can develop to their full potential.

A truly historic moment.

Chapter 1
What is a red brain?

ALAN, A YOUNG GRADUATE employed in a research department, found himself suddenly flustered as the head of department approached his desk. His heart began to thump and a strange feeling began welling up inside. He thought, "What have I done?" and his last few days' work flashed through his mind.

Margaret was a very competent deputy principal in a large girls' school, the school where she had been a student herself. She had a meeting with the father of a girl in year eleven, a likable and popular young woman, but easily distracted in class. Margaret expected a business-like meeting and so was not concerned. However, upon seeing the girl's father, Margaret felt a sudden twinge of anxiety and her mind started racing; she blurted out her good morning, then felt she had been too abrupt but it was too late to change it. She worried that the meeting was getting off on the wrong foot, but she could not think straight.

Both Alan and Margaret, successful as they are, are experiencing "red brain" events. Something in their environment − a teacher-like figure for Alan, a male authority figure for Margaret − has triggered memories from the past with attached negative feelings. These memories − probably subconscious − have set off a physical response that begins with an upwelling of emotion, and which narrows their focus (onto themselves), limits their ability to think and gives rise to negative self-talk. The net effect is to reduce their ability to engage fully with another person and to behave to their full capacity. They lack choice in their responses; they can only handle simple tasks; and will tend to generalise their negative experience.

As we will see, almost all of us operate in two brain states. In one, which I call the "blue brain", we are at our best: confident, generous, receptive to ideas, empathic and collaborative, creative, motivated and productive; we achieve and empower others to achieve; we do more together than we could alone; we intuitively know what is right and we have the courage to do it despite the consequences. In the other, the "red brain", we are well below our best. In the red brain, we lose access to our brain's cerebral cortex − the "higher" or "thinking" brain, operating instead from the more primitive areas or "lower" brain (more on this in chapter 3).

The following account of road rage by Frank Robson is a classic and spectacular example of the red brain taking over and driving us toward unhelpful outcomes.

He won't move over. He's in the overtaking lane, driving under the speed limit, but he won't budge. Assuming he's just another Oblivious One, I flash my lights. No response. When I flash again he hits the brakes, so I back off. Then he raises a middle finger and holds it before his rear-vision mirror.

Okay, not oblivious.

A gap appears in the inside lane, so I indicate a turn and move left to pass him on that side. He swerves across in front of me then brakes again, the finger still held motionless above his left shoulder.

It's the finger, more than anything, that gets me going. "You f---ing silly prick," I say aloud. My voice sounds thick and strange, and I can feel a chemical fizz in my veins. It's a weekday afternoon, I'm almost home and have no reason to hurry, yet it suddenly seems imperative that I show this idiot a clean pair of heels.

But each time I change lanes he cuts me off. Then, just before the multi-lane section ends, I feint left, floor it and roar past on the right before he has time to react. Glimpsed in passing, he looks about 25, his otherwise unremarkable face twisted by fury. (Why is he so pissed off? I have no idea, but for some reason seeing his anger increases my own.) For a moment we snarl at one another like dogs through a fence, and then he's behind me and we're in a 60km/h zone.

Har! Cop that, you mad little Millennial bastard!

But he isn't going to cop it. In fact — Jesus Christ! — he's overtaking me, almost forcing oncoming traffic off the road, then cutting in so abruptly I have to brake to avoid a collision. He slows to a crawl and his arm comes out the window and jabs across the roof towards the grass verge on our left. He wants to fight.

These are the moments when lives change. When warnings of catastrophe — of injury, death, prison, anguish, grief, penury — should pound like drums in our brains. When, according to experts, we should "remember our common humanity" and exercise forgiveness, or take deep calming breaths, or play soothing music, or speak to ourselves in "friendly, reassuring" tones.

But, let's face it, real anger drops its pants and moons such conventional wisdom. Depending on our personal reserves of the stuff, it can blind us to everything but the need to deal with whoever has wronged us so badly. Even when muted by fear it provides no sane plan, just a furious sense of indignation.

This is pretty much my condition when I pull up behind my fellow rager. Incredibly, all I have in mind is the delivery of a scathing lecture, but before I'm even out the door the other driver is sprinting towards me with a steel steering lock. Boom! The driver's side window explodes, showering me with fragments. I shove the door open, forcing him back, and stumble out.

When he raises the steering lock above my head, I grab it with both hands and hang on. So does he. We stagger about like this for a while, neither of us saying a word, watched impassively from the footpath by an enormous Pacific Islander with a flowery shopping bag on his arm. Moment by moment the absurdity of the situation builds until, visited at last by a coherent thought, I call to the onlooker, "Hey mate, could you help me get this thing off this maniac?"

The big guy puts down his bag, steps across and plucks the weapon from our hands with ridiculous ease. The kid bolts, leaps in his car and roars off. Knees rubbery and heart pounding, I sag against my own vehicle, suddenly aware of all the idiot impulses that have controlled me for the past few minutes. Not for the first time, only a propensity for farce has saved me from my 64-year-old self.

Sydney Morning Herald, 9 June 2018

When the red brain triggers

When the red brain triggers it prepares our body for fight or flight. We respond physically in three ways: we are overwhelmed with emotion; our focus narrows; and we get into a negative thinking cycle.

Triggering may happen in response to a person, an event, an idea or new information that challenges our beliefs. It is most likely to occur when we feel threatened in some way: when we feel unsafe, unvalued, judged, not listened to, that things are unfair or ambiguous or uncertain. In these conditions, we pull up memories of previous, similar situations. We may have lost the visual or motor aspects of the memory, retaining only the negative feeling. This first memory can call up others, causing a cascade of memories and hence of emotions.

Emotion

This flood of negative feeling is the main indication that the red brain has triggered (recall Frank Robson noticing "the chemical fizz in my veins"). To feed this swelling emotion, the older parts of the brain need resources – oxygen and glucose – which become diverted from the advanced parts of our brain via the left hemisphere into the older or sub-cortical regions of the brain. The emotion can be anger (fight), fear (flight) or a combination of both. These feelings can be overwhelming.

As we will see in chapter 2, recognising the welling emotion and allowing it to subside before it takes hold of us is an important step in being able to effectively manage our red brains.

Narrowing of focus

When the red brain triggers our focus narrows – physically, relationally and in our thinking. Physically, we lose peripheral vision and our attention is restricted to about one and a half degrees around the main axis of our eyesight. We have a physically narrower focus for attention.

We become narrower in terms of our connections. Imagine the self at the centre of a circle, surrounded by family and friends. Further out are colleagues and, beyond them, the broader community. We generally engage with and think about people across this circle. In the red brain, however, our focus shrinks back to the centre; we become self-focused.

In the red brain, our thinking becomes more backward looking, more negative, more closed, more black-and-white. We tend to justify and defend our position, and to generalise – thinking things like "this always happens to me".

Rumination

The third effect that we experience is an increase in rumination. We keep going over and over in our minds the same situation – typically the events that have caused the red brain to trigger – and engage in negative self-talk. In the absence of anger, we may feel deflated, worthless and hopeless – that things will always be like this. We tend to feel a victim, or deserving of whatever bad thing has happened. Conversely, anger can lead to extreme loss of control and violent action; if controlled, it can lead to internal "seething" as our focus narrows and rumination kicks in.

Research by Moore and Windcrest in 2002 showed that rumination is the form of self-attention most closely related to depressive symptoms. Shannon Kolakowski, who wrote *When depression hurts your relationship*, points out that the vast majority of thoughts during rumination are, at best, random and, at worst, destructive; and that ninety-five per cent of our thoughts are simply replaying past events or other random memories.

Chronic rumination is linked to anxiety as well as to the onset of depression. Although the primary driver of anxiety is worry rather than rumination, when we ruminate we are more likely to start worrying. Similarly, if we worry we are more likely to fall into rumination. Rumination, then, is linked to poor wellbeing.

The more we play a scenario over in our minds, the more likely it is that the scenario will occur again in the future. For example, my red brain might trigger during an interaction with a child. If I ruminate over the interaction, I am likely to recall whatever triggered my red brain the next time I see the child – which will trigger my red brain again. In effect, rumination adds another set of memories with negative feelings attached, which reinforces the original trigger. The more we ruminate on something the more likely it is that the same situation will occur again.

Isabel had been a primary school teacher for five years. She looked forward to getting to know each new class and watching them grow in ability through the year. Isabel got on easily with most students but as she saw Jared she felt a twinge of dislike. There was something about the way he talked, sort of out of the side of his mouth, and he had an odd laugh. She dismissed the feeling as she switched her attention to other new students. As the year progressed, however, the feeling about Jared continued and she found herself being a little harsher and colder with him than with the other students. Half way through the year, she realised that the other students had noticed her attitude to Jared; some of them were picking on him and even looking to her for affirmation when they did it. Isabel could not shake the feeling of dislike that she had for Jared and recognised that she was treating him differently. It felt wrong, but she could not stop. It was clear that Jared also knew by now that she did not like him, and he was falling behind in his work.

Taking an instant dislike to someone has little to do with the other person and a lot to do with us. Something in the other person triggers a memory or response that cascades and causes us to treat the other person differently. This is the red brain at work.

Recall that the red brain triggering is preparing our body for fight or flight, flooding it with chemicals that make us ready to respond and resist injury. But we were designed to be in such a position only very rarely. In normal circumstances, these chemicals – which can persist in our blood stream for as long as a month – dissipate and the body returns to normal. With frequent triggering of the red brain these chemicals are chronically present, generating long-term health issues as well as shorter-term issues such as difficulty in sleeping.

Having a red brain that we do not know how to control is, increasingly, a liability in today's world: damaging to both our physical and mental health. Our first step in managing the red brain is to learn how we can get out of it again, once it has taken us over.

Chapter 2

How to get out of the red brain I – immediate steps

I WAS IN MY EARLY THIRTIES and studying German as part of an MBA. While I was studious and excelled in class, some other students attended only the minimum number of classes required to graduate from the MBA program. In one class I found my red brain triggering when a sporty American football player – a big guy – arrived. Suddenly, I could not say anything right. My teacher, I could see, was surprised: her best student was barely able to function.

Some years later, in Australia, I noticed that Australian rules football players would often trigger my red brain – in particular, a commentator and former player who I often saw on television. I had played rugby at school and believed that the triggers dated from that time, but I had no explicit memories of how these red brain triggers had been formed.

However, it is possible to prevent ourselves falling completely into the red brain when it triggers. Using strategies to reduce my red brain triggering, I learned systematically to neutralise the triggers until I could watch this commentator talk about football without my red brain triggering at all.

Chapter 1 described the three physical responses that occur when our red brain triggers: we experience an upwelling of emotion, our focus narrows and we fall into rumination. To lift ourselves out of the red brain, we can apply three strategies to each of these responses: that is, there are nine possible things that we can do. Getting ourselves out of the red brain is like pulling ourselves out of wet cement; we need all the help we can possibly get, so having multiple strategies is essential.

Red brain triage

What can we do immediately our red brain triggers? As soon as we feel the welling up of negative emotions, we must act. We need to physically shift our attention away from the three effects that are all beginning and growing in strength. This is like a paramedic's work on a wounded patient: the first priority is to stop the bleeding. When the red brain triggers, we need to widen our focus, stop the rumination and wind down the negative feelings.

Move to widen your focus

The first key action is to physically move. Get up, move your body, walk; anything that simply moves you. This helps to reverse the physical narrowing of your focus. Looking at more distant objects, gazing out of the window, or engaging your peripheral vision by looking at things from the corner of your eye will also help.

I have a very embarrassing example of not moving when my red brain triggered. I was in the military a long time ago, based in Germany and, on this night, was duty officer. In the duty officer's overnight room was just room for a single bed, a small table and a telephone. My role was to sleep there and, if the telephone rang, listen to the code word and take appropriate action. Most of the time the code word indicated that everything was fine and no action was to be taken; but, on this night, I was required to pass this code on to others. When the code came through, my red brain triggered; I became paralysed. I was in this tiny room, I had just been woken up, I could not move, and I did not pass on the code word. This led to a whole bunch of unhappy consequences, not least my embarrassment at messing up an apparently simple task. At the time, I didn't know that getting up and moving would have helped me; being restricted by the smallness of the room, I remained inactive – disabled by my red brain.

To stop our focus shrinking back to ourselves, we need to shift attention outwards. Try to focus on someone else: a colleague who is passing, or a photograph of family. If someone you are with has triggered your red brain, try to look into their eyes (this can be hard) or at least at their ears or their hair. (Avoid looking at their mouth, which will tend to encourage the narrowing of focus.) The key is to pay attention to something other than yourself.

Engage in something else

As rumination begins to take hold, we engage in negative self-talk as we replay events in our minds – even continuing or modifying the narrative to justify our actions.

To stop rumination in its tracks, engage fully in another activity. When we read a good book there is no rumination. When we watch a good film, there is no rumination. Anything that fully engages our attention is a way to shift out of rumination. It is worth having to hand a poem, a prayer or another form of inspiring text that you can pull out and read. You may need to read the first few sentences more than once until your attention is fully on the text, but once you are engaged the rumination will stop, at least for the moment.

Distract yourself

Rising negative feeling is the key indicator of the red brain triggering; to shift our attention, we can distract ourselves from the negative feelings. Here are some examples of how to do this:

If you feel deflated, try looking at something that inspires you: it could be a poster on your wall (that you keep for such occasions), or pictures of your children or another person close to you. Look at something that will generate a positive emotion rather than a negative one.

If you feel worthless, recall a time when you felt good about yourself; when you did succeed. It could be winning a race, delivering a satisfying piece of work or solving a difficult problem – anything that distracts you from the negative feeling.

If anger is part of the negative emotion, focusing on your breathing or counting up to ten can help to distract you from that negative emotion.

Although it is hard to remember it in the moment, this emotion is simply a feeling: it is temporary and, at some time in the near future, you will no longer feel it; you will be back to normal.

So, the immediate response is to shift ourselves: we move, we engage, we distract. These are all effective ways of getting us out of the initial red brain triggering that has taken place.

Bringing the blue brain back with analysis

As we saw in chapter 1, when the red brain triggers, resources move into the older parts of the brain so we are ready for fight or flight. Our body is also flooded with chemicals to prepare it for what might happen next. These chemicals do not immediately disappear, so the red brain will persist beyond our immediate first aid. Thus, it is easier to fall into the red zone than it is to get out of it again.

The next step is to move resources back to the modern part of the brain, and so quieten down the older parts systematically. To do that we have to engage in activities that are only possible in the blue brain, meaning: we have to engage in higher-order thinking activities. The easiest way to do this is to begin analysis. This will move us back towards the blue brain in and of itself, as can any output of the analysis.

Examine your thinking

Start by examining how your focus has narrowed, particularly around thinking. What is my thinking? Is it positive? Is it negative? Am I being defensive? Examine who you're focusing on: Am I thinking about myself? About those close to me? My colleagues? Examine where you're directing attention: Am I listening to what is being said or being done around me? Or am I listening to my own thoughts?

To analyse our focus, we must use the more advanced parts of the brain; by engaging this region, we shift resources back from the lower brain to the higher brain, which needs to happen if we are to get back to the blue brain.

Describe your emotions

The strategy in analysing our emotion is to describe what we are feeling as accurately as possible. Am I feeling angry, hostile, or just irritated? Do I feel annoyed, or aggravated? Am I exasperated or simply displeased? Am I cross? Am I fuming or enraged or just ill-tempered? Am I incensed or indignant or affronted? Do I feel resentful? Sulky? Or disgruntled?

The research shows quite clearly that the more detail we can use in describing our emotions, the better we can manage our emotions. In short, the more rapidly our negative feelings will subside. The effort required to precisely identify our feelings puts a major call on the advanced parts of the brain and, to do this, we need to shift resources there. So, the more words we have, the better the control we have over our feelings. A longer-term strategy is to build up a list of words that allow us to describe in detail what feelings we are experiencing.

We can also split out our feelings into different components. For example, I once made a major error and my red brain triggered as a result. My analysis went something like this: I made a mistake, and I feel bad about it. I could have got it right, but for some reason I did not. But what does "feeling bad" mean? I feel that the outcome could have been different, so it means I did not perform so well. I feel guilt (because I could have got it right); I feel I am not as good as I thought. I have a feeling of inadequacy, of being inept.

The mistake was also public, so I feel embarrassed and even a little humiliated; do I feel ashamed? It is probably embarrassment because I fell short of my own standards (I am proud that I do not make mistakes). After having made a mistake that is public I feel embarrassed. Finally, I feel annoyed and irritated that Ted brought this up in such a casual way, which is what triggered the red brain event in the first place.

By describing my feelings in detail, and teasing them out to identify the separate aspects, I can gain greater control over those feelings. Moreover, the examination process is activating my blue brain.

Evaluate ruminating thoughts

Rumination is strongly linked to both depression and anxiety, so continuing to ruminate is not helpful at all. Simply noticing that we are ruminating helps us to stop. We evaluate what is occurring in our minds: I can see that I am replaying events; I can hear my internal self-talk. To avoid reinforcing (and therefore perpetuating) this memory, I need to bring the rumination to a close.

To step out of rumination, I can evaluate the thoughts swirling through my mind and identify those that are linked to the red brain event. Examples of ruminating thoughts might be: "this is all so unfair" or "this always happens to me". The act of identifying ruminating thoughts from the trigger event uses the blue brain.

Through analysis (of our thinking, emotions and rumination), we re-engage our higher brains. Not only does this shift resources out of the primitive regions that activated in the red brain event; it also sets us up to re-establish our blue brain state through a final strategy: reframing.

Seeing things differently

The final steps we can take in this immediate response to a red-brain event is to reframe what we are experiencing: rather than seeing our experience through a red brain lens – negative and narrow – we can interpret it in a more positive and expansive way.

Reimagine your focus

Reimagining is a powerful way to shift our focus: we reframe our experience in a positive, rather than negative, light. Here's an example of how we can reimagine our thinking: Instead of viewing this situation as a setback, I can think of it as an opportunity. The mistake I made has been distressing for me but perhaps it is a blessing in disguise. Without such a wake-up call I would not be thinking so carefully about my work, but perhaps I should. Careful thinking leads me to the beginning of a shift in the way I do my work. Reimagining the situation to see the positive aspect helps us to get out of negative thinking patterns.

What would an observer of this incident make of it all? Rather than being part of the event that has just taken place, I can reimagine it from a different viewpoint. A third-party perspective is dispassionate; focused more on the facts than the emotions. We can only take this view from within the blue brain, so reimagining our focus helps to keep us in a blue brain state.

When my physical attention has been narrowed down to the here and now, thinking about the upsetting event in the context of a much longer timeframe can help me to reimagine the event as being quite minor in the scheme of things.

I like the story about the first spaceship that went to the moon. Apparently, it was off course ninety-seven per cent of the time. Every time it was off course was an opportunity to bring it back onto a truer course. I used this analogy during my own experience in building a start-up business from scratch. When you are building a business – as when you're going to the moon – you know what you are aiming for but you will keep drifting off course as problems crop up, and you do not know the full effect of each action you take to fix them.

After a while I began to realise that, while I thought I was heading in the right direction, I did not really know where I was until something went wrong. Then I could take corrective action to get more on the right track again. It was exactly like getting the spaceship back onto course. I began to look forward to things going wrong because, if several weeks passed without anything going wrong, I'd know I was drifting away from where I needed to go, but wouldn't know how far away I was. Only when something went wrong was I able to make the necessary adjustment.

This became a powerful reimagining hack that allowed me to fool the red brain completely within the context of things going wrong in the business. My red brain no longer triggered, and I was at my best in resolving problems as they arose.

Redirect your thinking

Rather than replaying the past, it is more useful to imagine the future. By redirecting our internal narrative away from the past and towards the more positive events of the future, we can further reduce rumination. I feel negative about how things went; but how would I have felt if things had gone well? Then: What could I do to achieve this next time? This strategy helps us begin to find solutions – which by their nature are about the future – instead of dwelling on the past.

Reframing can be particularly helpful in handling our negative feelings that arise when the red brain triggers. To explain this, I need to digress and look a little at the history of how we view feelings and emotions. You can skip this section if you are not interested, and get right into relabelling, below.

EMOTIONS ARE NOT WHAT WE THINK – A SHORT DIGRESSION

In 1872, Charles Darwin published *The expression of the emotions in man and animals,* in which he argued that each of our emotions is associated with unique physical characteristics: an elevated heart rate, moistening of the skin, contraction of various muscles in our face would be unique indications of anger, for example. Coming thirteen years after his seminal work, *On the origin of species*, this book had widespread impact, and his theory on emotional expression has persisted in popular imagination. However, there is simply no scientific evidence to support this view.

An explanation that fits the evidence much more closely than Darwin's theory is the theory of constructed emotions, which argues that we have a series of sensations, which the brain interprets and categorises as specific emotions. It hypothesises that we develop categories of emotions over our lives. For example, within the category we call "anger" are many instances of anger that we have seen or experienced. As a young child, we might see our mother shout an expletive then explain that she got angry because another driver cut in in front of us. From a very early age we hear the word anger; we see and experience instances of it, which begin to populate the anger category. As we go through life, we categorise thousands of instances of anger, happiness, anxiety, jealousy, and many other emotions.

Curiously, the theory of constructed emotion corresponds more closely to Darwin's ideas on evolution than do his ideas on emotion: while there are many different instances of anger, there is no essence of anger; no set of physical characteristics that are unique to anger. We are simply interpreting what we see in others or feel ourselves, based on a lifetime of precedents.

Lev Kuleshov (1899–1970) was a filmmaker who used editing techniques including the cut (an abrupt, but usually minor film transition from one sequence to another) to emotionally influence the audience, a principle known as the Kuleshov effect. He edited a short film in which the same shot of Tsarist matinee idol Ivan Mosjoukine with an expressionless face was alternated with various other images (a plate of soup, a girl in a coffin, a woman on a divan). The film was shown to an audience, who believed that Mosjoukine's expression was different each time he appeared, showing hunger, grief or desire, depending on whether he was "looking at" the plate of soup, the girl in the coffin, or the woman on the divan.

Vsevolod Pudovkin (who later claimed to have been the co-creator of the experiment) described in 1929 how the audience "raved about the acting... the heavy pensiveness of his mood over the forgotten soup, were touched and moved by the deep sorrow with which he looked on the dead child and noted the lust with which he observed the woman. But we knew that in all three cases the face was exactly the same." The implication is that viewers brought their own emotional reactions to this sequence of images, and attributed those reactions to the actor, investing his impassive face with their own feelings.

This type of effect is not limited to intercutting film and juxtaposing distinct images. The background of a still photograph can change how we emotionally "read" a face. We think that we are seeing emotions in the face, but we are influenced by the whole image (which can, in turn, change our categorisation of the emotion we think we are seeing).

A further example is about judges who were hearing prisoners' applications for parole. The judges would listen to applicants all day, and determine whether they thought each person was sincere in their remorse and desire to avoid criminal activity in the future. The judges believed that their long experience had given them good acumen. However, research then showed that, in the hour before lunch, judges were turning down applicants at a far higher rate, statistically, than in the morning or afternoon. After more detailed analysis, the researchers realised that the judges were getting hungry in the hour before lunch, which caused a negative feeling. Judges thought they had a good handle on an applicant's sincerity, yet simply being hungry changed the quality of their feelings towards the applicants, and the judges' interpretation.

Relabel your feeling

An effective way to manage the negative feelings that arise when the red brain triggers is to relabel. The first step is to make the shift from "I *am* angry" or "I *am* anxious" to "I *have* angry feelings" or "I *have* anxious feelings". The first relabelling makes clear that this emotion is not *me*; it is something that I have. You can apply this to the very detailed understanding of your feelings that emerged from your analysis, described earlier in the chapter.

We can then relabel feelings as something else. There is a nice piece of research around students coming to an exam: because their hearts are hammering, they say, "I must be anxious". But equally the students could say, "an exam is coming, my heart is hammering: I must be excited".

Clearly, the same feeling could be an instance of either anxiety or excitement. Or indeed it could be an instance of anticipation: "I have been waiting for this exam so long, I am ready; my anticipation is causing my heart to hammer". The research showed that students who went into the exam having relabelled their hammering heart as excitement performed better than those who went in having labelled their hammering heart as anxiety.

Relabelling can have a very significant impact on how we perform. You can see now why I digressed around the theory that emotions are constructed: under the classical theory, a hammering heart could not be interpreted as one emotion or another, but would classify it as anxiety, full stop. Using the theory of constructed emotions, we can interpret feelings in a number of different ways and relabel a negative feeling to something else – anxiety to excitement, for example.

Feelings of worthlessness, for example, can be relabelled: "I am on a steep learning curve and it is quite normal to feel a little lost at the beginning of something. This does not mean that I am no good in general; but, because I am at the bottom of a steep learning curve, I do not know what to do at this point".

We could go further and recognise that when we learn something new, when we grow, when we move forward, we must leave earlier beliefs behind, and leaving stuff behind needs a period of grieving. What we are feeling could be relabelled as an instance of grieving, a perfectly natural feeling to have as we grow and develop. Relabelling is a powerful way of being able to reinterpret feelings in different ways, which helps us to move out of the red brain and back into the blue brain.

We have now covered nine key strategies. Though they can be used in any order that suits us, the "shift, analyse and reframe" progression makes logical sense. We can do this for each specific aspect: for instance, when we notice negative feelings as our red brain triggers, we can distract ourselves to shift away from the feelings; analyse exactly what we are feeling by describing them in as much detail as possible; then relabel those feelings to something that is more useful to us.

The bottom line is that when your red brain triggers, there is a lot that you can do to reduce its impact and get back onto an even keel as quickly as possible.

	Narrowed Focus	Negative Feelings	Rumination
Shift	Move	Distract	Engage
Analyse	Examine	Describe	Evaluate
Reframe	Re-imagine	Re-label	Re-direct

Nine strategies for getting out of the red brain

Chapter 3
Where the red brain comes from

HUMAN BRAINS, BEING LARGER and more complex than those of other organisms, take many years to develop fully. Compared with other animals, we have a long childhood, during which time, our brain transitions from a child mind into an adult mind state − all being well. However, if this transition is disrupted, the child mind may remain. The widespread use of reward and punishment to shape behaviour has contributed to the child mind (and, hence, the red brain) persisting into adulthood, notably, through the influence of parents and − over the last two hundred years − state compulsory schooling.

Our layered brains

The human evolutionary journey is visible in the structures of our body (particularly during foetal development, where we show the first signs of a tail, which disappears again; and webbed fingers, which then grow into hands); and of our brain.

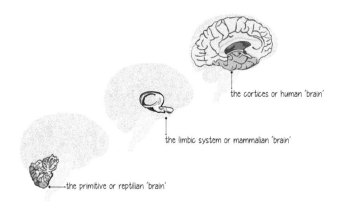

the cortices or human 'brain'

the limbic system or mammalian 'brain'

the primitive or reptilian 'brain'

The layered human brain

In the brain, we see three broad stages of evolution, layered in increasing complexity. The first stage – the area above and connected to the spinal cord – is the very primitive or "reptilian brain", which provides the automated responses characteristic of reptiles: seek food, procreate, and freeze, fight or flee when danger appears.

The second stage is the limbic system or "mammalian brain", above the first layer and in the middle of our brains. It is responsible for feelings and long-term memory, allowing members of a species to form relationships, for example: adults with their young; members of the group or herd with each other. Advantages include protection in numbers, learning from play, and watching successful adults and remembering what they do.

The third and largest layer is the cortices or "human brain" that envelops the other layers and enables most of what makes us distinctly human. Through the cortices, we have self-awareness, speech, the capacity to manage our impulses and instincts – and thus to make choices, and the capacity to imagine a future different from today and act to move towards it.

These layers are not separate. As each has evolved, they have become entwined so there are direct connections between the layers; for example, the "human" and "reptilian" brains are connected, which is how we can override our impulses and instincts and make choices.

A vast and complex network

The human brain is large relative to the human body. The adult brain, at an average of 1.5 kilograms, has eighty-six billion neurons and eighty-five billion non-neuronal cells. Neurons are the basic building block of the brain; through connections with other neurons, they create a dazzlingly complex and adaptable network: the foundation of our cognitive abilities.

Connections between neurons begin within a baby's brain once the production of neurons is complete and continues at an astonishingly high rate – thousands of connections per second – for about the first three years. There is evidence that babies begin with even more neurons, and that those not subsequently much used are re-absorbed into the body, particularly during adolescence. In adults, the average neuron has ten thousand connections and some neurons can have as many as a hundred thousand – so do the maths. Some connections that go into the body can be two metres long.

The cortices themselves are a split pair – left and right hemispheres – with connections taking place at their base via the corpus callosum, a wide band of fibres that connects the two hemispheres. The hemispheres are noticeably different in composition, the right hemisphere being a little larger and heavier, with connections between neurons tending to be longer; this hemisphere is deeply connected into the sub-cortical (lower) regions of the brain and into the body itself.

Otherwise there is essentially no lateralisation in the brain: we cannot point to an area that is specific to one hemisphere and say when you do that, or when you think this, it is that side of the brain that is doing it. Even speech, which is known to use two dedicated areas in the left hemisphere, intimately involves both hemispheres. So the human brain is a massive and complex interconnected network, which takes a long time to develop.

Childhood: a critical period of brain development

Due to the size of the brain, and the head that contains it, young humans are born before the brain is fully formed, so that the head can pass through the birth canal. Given the pain and damage that birth often entails, things are clearly being left to the last possible moment. As the brain grows in the womb, through childhood and into adulthood, it grows and matures in the order that it evolved. The very last parts are not fully developed until our mid-twenties.

This means that up until the age of about ten the parts of the brain that are in control, so to speak, are the more primitive parts – the reptilian and mammalian brains. The human brain is growing, and elements of its capabilities emerge at different stages, but the childhood mind is characterised by the reptilian and mammalian brains. In fact, up to the age of about two and a half, babies are surprisingly like puppies in both brain structure and behaviour; but they keep growing in capability, whilst a dog has reached its mental limits.

Children are self-centred and impulsive; they can handle simple tasks well, they respond to reward and punishment, their emotions tend to be overwhelming and they have no real ability to imagine a future different from today – if they are miserable today they will be miserable forever! This mind state stays in exclusive control for the first ten years of life.

From the age of about ten onwards, the adult mind state emerges, based on the whole brain.

The adult mind brings self-awareness, the ability to expand awareness through higher-order learning, the capacity to be social, and the ability to imagine, and then plan to achieve, a different future. Emotions are only one input and do not overwhelm; we are able to choose, and to defer gratification. When the adult mind is fully expressed we are confident, collaborative and creative.

At the most basic level we can say that education (Latin: *ex + ducere*, to lead out of) is the process of leading the child out of the childhood mind and into the adult mind. And this leading is necessary as the childhood mind has been in exclusive control for a decade and has no capacity to determine for itself that it should change. However, nature comes to the rescue by creating existential anxiety.

Leaving the childhood mind behind

Shortly after the emerging adult mind realises that it exists – becomes self-aware – it realises that there is the possibility of its non-existence: that it could die – indeed, that it is going to die. As this thought presents itself, the childhood mind goes frantic – I'm going to die! – and tries everything it knows in terms of fight and flight to avoid it, but the thought remains. Many people can remember around the age of about ten crying themselves to sleep or desperately trying to stay awake for fear that they would not wake up again. This can last for six weeks or so before we find a way to manage it.

This is existential anxiety: existential because it is a part of our very existence. Whether we like it or not, accept it or not, we are going to die. The presence of this anxiety ensures that a change will occur when the adult mind emerges. Reflect for a moment: the childhood mind has been in control for a decade and, as it has no perception that an adult mind state exists, it naturally wants to continue in control. It is existential anxiety that ensures movement.

If this anxiety is not alleviated then, as they grow, the child will take increasingly desperate measures to escape it. At one extreme these measures can be highly creative; at the other, highly destructive – the most extreme being suicide. Most will be antisocial. For the wellbeing of the child and the good order of society, this anxiety needs to be allayed.

The most natural way to relieve the child's existential anxiety is to help them to move into the adult mind – which is where we develop the courage to go on while accepting that we will die – and to let the childhood mind fade away.

Without the childhood mind reacting so strongly to the idea that the organism is going to die, our fight-flight mechanism is not triggered when we begin to contemplate our own mortality.

The move to the adult mind, with the associated fading away of the childhood mind, may occur seamlessly when the child is in the presence of at least one adult who offers unconditional acceptance to the child, accepts them for who they are, listens to them, and believes in their capacity to grow; and when this takes place in a safe environment.

When this smooth shift from child to adult occurs, we grow into adults who operate in the adult mind. However, all too often, the path from child mind to adult mind is influenced by other forces, which interfere with the transition. Going back to our simple model of education as the process of leading the child out of the childhood mind and into the adult mind, there are two other possible outcomes: the least desirable is that the child actually remains in the childhood mind – that is, the adult mind never emerges; the second is that the adult mind emerges alongside the childhood mind – that is, the childhood mind persists into adulthood, while the adult mind develops in parallel.

Another possibility: remaining in the childhood mind

During the nineteenth century, education in the Western world (and regions influenced by colonial powers) was characterised by harsh discipline and rote learning. As a result, a large proportion of the population never moved out of the childhood mind. Why?

Harsh discipline keeps the fight-flight mechanism very much active; it instils in the child a belief that if they do as they are told they will be all right but, if they transgress in any way, they will be harshly punished. When existential anxiety arises, the child holds even more strongly onto this belief, which allays their anxiety so they can function.

Rote learning simplifies the massive neural network by laying down some responses that have been repeated so often that the brain automatically uses these when anything occurs. The flexibility and plasticity of the brain – its ability to change its network structure in response to changes in how we think – are both minimised.

BRAIN PATHWAYS

Our brains consist of networks of connected neurons along which electrical signals are relayed from neuron to neuron. When we use a series of connections frequently, our brains wrap the connections with an insulator (a fatty substance called myelin – the "white matter" of the brain, the "grey matter" being the neurons), which allows the signal to travel with less "leakage" into neighbouring neurons. The brain can wrap multiple layers of insulation around important pathways, making these responses reliable and very rapid. It is this process that allows sports people – tennis players for example – to respond so accurately after years of practice; it also explains why we become less precise in our actions – and our memories – with age, as the myelin sheaths begin to degrade.

Use of harsh discipline and rote learning produces habitual and obedient adults who are unable to act without someone in authority telling them what to do. This was ideal for large-scale armies and for the division of labour to be expanded on an industrial scale. Accordingly, this education model was widely adopted around the world in the nineteenth century, following its initial development in Prussia.

However, this form of education reached its sell-by date around the First World War, and lost its dominance in the period immediately after the Second World War; it had faded away by the early 1980s (if we measure its demise by the prohibitions on corporal punishment), earlier in some parts of the world.

A third possibility: the two-brain state

Along with their model of harsh discipline and rote learning, the Prussians also designed a system to educate the administrators, doctors, engineers: all those who would support the state. These people would require high levels of knowledge and the ability to apply that knowledge in practical ways.

Following the demise of the nineteenth-century model of education, this second model – originally designed for around five per cent of the Prussian population – expanded after the Second World War to become the dominant model by the 1970s. It would have shaped most people reading this book today. This twentieth-century form of education develops the adult mind. However, while not so harsh and regimented as its precursor, its use of controlled motivation – reward and punishment – means that it also allows the childhood mind to persist into adulthood: it gives rise to the two-brain state.

The blue brain is the adult mind which, when in operation, allows us to be at our best. The red brain, when triggered, gives us access only to the parts of the brain that the childhood mind had access to – the more primitive parts – and we can only act accordingly. The red brain triggers when we feel threatened in some way, physically or psychologically.

So twentieth-century education produces adults who are cognitively well developed – who can think – but are unable to question or challenge the status quo. As they get close to the boundary of what are acceptable thoughts, their childhood mind triggers, they are flooded with fear or anxiety and they retreat from the boundary.

The central promise of this type of education is: do as you are told, and you will have a good life. The welfare state was introduced and expanded in parallel as this form of education began to dominate. The welfare state gave us pensions when we were too old to work, unemployment benefits if we lost our job and affordable medical care if we were sick. Anxieties about the future were allayed and we could focus on simply doing our work.

The role of controlled motivation

A great deal of personal and professional development today is about how we can stay in the blue brain and avoid triggering the red brain, despite living and working in increasingly challenging environments.

But why doesn't the red brain just fade away when we leave school? This is a good question. The childhood mind first persists into adulthood because adults in general, and educators in our schools, model the two brains to children and use controlled motivation as the way to get children to behave and to do their school work.

The average parent or educator demonstrates to the child that: if you do what I want you to do I will be good to you, but if you *don't*, I will get emotional and intimidate you or humiliate you in some way. When the child conforms to the adult's wishes, she or he can operate in the emerging blue brain, the ideal mind state for higher-order learning and healthy development to take place. However, when the child does not conform in a school setting then the teacher might humiliate them in front of the class, triggering the child's red brain; in response, he or she retreats into the childhood mind, and the other children in the class retreat as well – maybe not as far, but enough to keep the childhood mind alive.

Throughout our upbringing and schooling this process goes on, so that young adults emerge with two brain states: red brain and blue brain.

But once out of the school environment, why can't we just let the red brain fade away – as it is supposed to do? If anything, there is more anxiety, more red brain triggering than before. The next chapter will address this conundrum.

Chapter 4
Why the red brain persists

ANOTHER MECHANISM BUILT into our schooling systems creates the conditions for the red brain to persist beyond school.

We learned in chapter 3 that our brains are dynamic: the neural network can and does change in structure, particularly during childhood, and often-used neural pathways are insulated to make them more efficient. The style in which we are educated can critically influence the way our brains learn to respond – and which hemisphere they respond with.

In this chapter, we will see how our current school system encourages left hemisphere preferencing, and how this in turn encourages the red brain to remain active into adulthood. But first, it's important to understand the significance of the split brain. We have already seen that the cortices of our brains are split into two hemispheres: left and right. Though there is little, if any, lateralisation in the brain, it does not mean the two hemispheres don't play different roles.

Significance of the split brain

Picture a small bird – a sparrow, perhaps – hopping around on the ground pecking for food. Birds, like many animals, have split brains: one hemisphere focuses on finding food, while the other scans for threats. The bird's right eye – connected to its left hemisphere – looks for seed among grains of dirt: it takes a very local, detailed focus, searching for what is familiar (a seed). Meanwhile, the other eye – connected to its right hemisphere – scans for possible threats. It takes a more global view, looking for discrepancies – a shadow, for example.

These two activities – maintaining awareness of the wider environment, and focusing closely to exploit the very local – are two quite different ways of looking at the world. Both are essential for survival: to live and grow, an organism must be able to use resources from within its environment for food and shelter. It must also be aware of its surroundings so it can respond to threats. It is common to see small birds hop face-about so the appropriate eye can see potential food or a potential threat.

For the bird to be successful, it is important that a response to something unexpected takes precedence over exploitation. If the bird's right hemisphere, through its left eye, detects an approaching shadow – a potential predator homing in – then this latest information should dictate what happens next. At this point we do not want the left hemisphere to say, "Oh, another seed, let me just get that" and that view to prevail. For the bird's survival (to eat another seed in the future) it must move away from the possible threat. We see this very clearly in birds, as they will hop away from a perceived threat and then come back to find the seed a moment later.

The more general conclusion here is that, in split-brain organisms, the natural order is for the right hemisphere to lead – to navigate through a dangerous world – and for the left hemisphere ably to assist in exploiting the world for its survival. Humans are vastly more evolved than birds, but the same basic principle applies. When something new occurs, it is in the global view and we want the right hemisphere to lead in responding.

How our brain responds to sensory information

When sensory information is presented to our brains, both hemispheres receive it. One hemisphere puts its hand up and says, "I'll take the lead on this", and sends an inhibitory signal to the other hemisphere through the corpus callosum. There are many things that go naturally to one hemisphere or the other. If I hold up a hammer (or any type of tool) the left hemisphere will put its hand up. If I hold up a musical instrument the right will. Both hammers and musical instruments fit into categories that our ancestors would have recognised, so our brains have evolved knowing which hemisphere should take the lead.

For many other things, things which exist today and did not in the past, it can be random as to which hemisphere puts its hand up. When we are young, one hemisphere randomly puts its hand up and then, next time (because it did it last time), it puts its hand up again. To some extent this explains the lack of lateralisation in the brain. Two people can respond to the same stimulus with different hemispheres and so different parts of their brain would light up under an fMRI scanner, the standard tool for brain imaging of this type.

This means that sometimes it can be the wrong hemisphere for what we want to do. Wrong in the sense of not being optimised for the task it has volunteered for. I have an everyday example of this, which intensely irritates my wife, and had been a puzzle to me for many years. When I drive somewhere I have difficulty in remembering the route I am taking, even if I have taken it many times before (and I do mean many times: I can drive the same route for a year but if I go on holiday, I will have difficulty when I get back). I will come to a corner and expect that the road around the corner to be such and such, but when I turn the corner it is completely different.

The reason is that, when I drive, my left hemisphere puts its hand up to handle navigation – completely inappropriately. Because it categorises information, the left hemisphere will group similar scenes in memory, rather than arranging them in their spatial sequence. When I see the corner coming up, my mind pulls up an image that is similar, rather than pulling up the next image in sequence; when I go around the corner, the image I expect is the wrong one. I can override this: when I am in a completely unfamiliar place and must get back to my hotel, I pay proper attention and record the scenes in sequence; it is just my default that is unhelpful. GPSs are a godsend!

For many things, having the "wrong" hemisphere respond is just an irritating quirk. However, there are situations where it has more serious consequences – using the left hemisphere for engaging with another person, for example. That hemisphere is optimised for exploitation of things, not for connecting with people, so using it in this situation can cause us to have very unsatisfying relationships.

So, let's look a bit more closely at each hemisphere to see what characteristics they have.

The left hemisphere

The left hemisphere is optimised for exploitation of its local environment. Focused on its own wellbeing, it is selfish, and it is competitive. Finding food is one of its main drivers; food is scarce, so it wants to get the food that is available before someone or something else does.

To do this efficiently, the left hemisphere creates a static worldview, one that represents (or re-presents) the real world. This worldview is made up of parts put together rather than seeing the world all in one go, so to speak, which allows the left hemisphere to focus on just a small part, if necessary. With such a static view, it can then create rules, routines and automatic processes that make it very efficient at doing things that it has done before.

To know that it is handling something familiar, the left hemisphere will immediately and automatically compare and then categorise new images, ideas or thoughts. As we have seen in the example of my driving navigation, it categorises by similarity rather than by any other criteria, so that it can readily find other images that are like what it is now seeing. When presented with new information, the left hemisphere will bring images or memories into the conscious mind of similar things that it has experienced before, to satisfy itself that the new information is familiar and, therefore, that it knows how to handle it.

During this process of comparison, the left hemisphere sends a signal to suppress the senses so that we momentarily stop being aware of additional new information. Quite literally, we do not hear or see anything going on around us; so if this happens to be something important, we miss it. This gap is usually unnoticeable but can extend to several seconds if the new information or image requires some reworking to fit into the left hemisphere's world-view, or if the memories trigger a new thought and we follow this new input within our own minds. We have all had experiences where we realise we have not heard a thing that was said for the last few seconds (or more!). This suppression of our senses is most likely to occur with something we are already familiar with, as it is the familiar that will pull up most memories for our review. It can also occur when we are listening to someone who is familiar to us: we expect them to say something we know – and when they say something unfamiliar, we must work hard to make it fit, or discard it if it doesn't.

The left hemisphere stays with what it knows: it is receptive to things that are familiar – that will fit into its worldview – but will ignore discrepancies altogether if it cannot make them fit, so new information runs the risk of being ignored. It will also make up parts that are missing – make assumptions, for example.

This hemisphere is verbal: it uses words to articulate

– either in our heads, or out loud to other people (or things: we talk to pets or swear at recalcitrant computer equipment). Verbal communication tends to be about something; in a sense, it's just another form of exploitation. We can manipulate things with our fingers and we can talk verbally about them.

Emotions in the left hemisphere tend to be superficial; this hemisphere is not deeply connected into the body so cannot feel acutely how the whole organism is responding to external events. The image of the left hemisphere that comes to mind is of a very efficient but slightly anxious manager, who has no time for anything but shallow emotion as they organise and direct all the things that are happening around them.

This also means that the left hemisphere has no control over the sub-cortical regions of the brain: it cannot control the red brain when it triggers. The left hemisphere can be happily doing its thing when the red brain triggers and bang! Sudden waves of hopelessness wash over it and the self-talk goes negative.

The left hemisphere and "flow"

At its very best the left hemisphere goes into "flow", where time seems to pass without us realising: we do not notice feeling hungry and are immune to external distractions. In this state we can get a lot of detailed work done.

It takes about 15 consecutive minutes of focus before you can fully engage in a task, before you are "in flow". Research shows that people in a flow state are five times more productive than they otherwise would be. When you click out of your work because you get an impulse to check the news, Facebook, a sports score or whatever, this pulls you out of flow – meaning you need another 15 minutes of continuous focus to re-enter the flow state.

I am quite adept at designing spreadsheets to present information in a variety of ways from raw data. When I sit down to design a spreadsheet then I soon go into flow and will work for two or three hours on something that is familiar and challenging at the same time. Familiar, because I have done this many times before; challenging, as I need to create a certain effect and must work out how to do that within the limitations of the format. I feel, and know, that I am being very productive when I do this. Software programming lends itself to the same flow state, with programmers commonly doing mammoth sessions, writing code that they are very familiar with to achieve new effects.

The knowledge that the left hemisphere acquires is of the transportable kind: we can take in a fact or procedure and then give it out again in an exam or demonstration. This type of knowledge is not unique to us and is the sort of knowledge that can be found through an Internet search.

So, the left hemisphere has its capabilities that make it very effective in handling the routine, the day-to-day, with just a small amount of incremental challenge.

The right hemisphere

The right hemisphere is optimised for connecting outside of itself and finding patterns in the connections it makes. This hemisphere is deeply connected into the sub-cortical regions of the brain and the body more generally. These deep connections explain why empathy is seated in this hemisphere: we can feel what others are feeling; first, because we can feel; and, second, because we can observe what is outside of us without judgement. The right hemisphere does not compare and categorise.

The right hemisphere travels through a world that is always new; it expects to find the unfamiliar and thus is not fazed by it. In fact, the right hemisphere will look for discrepancies – things that do not fit. We have all had the experience of walking into a room, feeling something is different, and then having to look around to find that a piece of furniture has been moved. When it finds a discrepancy, the right hemisphere will strive to explain it. Something has changed; there is something new. Because of the structure of the right hemisphere, and its low rate of neuronal fatigue compared to the left hemisphere, it can see the world all in one go, in full three-dimensional colour, which gives it this ability to detect difference. From an evolutionary point of view this ability to detect a possible threat at its very first, faint appearance is indispensable.

The worldview of the right hemisphere comes from its latest understanding of how the world works; this view is continually updated as new information comes in and new patterns are identified. In that sense, the right hemisphere is very concrete in its worldview: it is based on what is happening now and it changes with time.

Communication, collaboration and caring

The right hemisphere is non-verbal but, as it is deeply connected into the body, it can communicate through feelings; in other words, through intuition: "this feels like the right thing to do". If you want to buy a house, the better strategy is to visit a range of houses and then buy the one that feels right. An inferior strategy is to write down a list of pros and cons for each house and then use logic to determine which is the best choice. The intuitive strategy works best because the right hemisphere takes in a lot more, and a wider range of, information, and processes it according to its innate desire to improve its life.

Gesture and music are other ways that the right hemisphere can communicate. The difference between a technically competent pianist and a super star is the level of communication that is taking place; we are moved by the great makers of music.

While the left hemisphere communicates about something (I–it), the right hemisphere's communication is with another being in the mode of I–thou. The I–thou communication brings in additional information, new perspectives, which we can incorporate into our own knowing.

The right hemisphere is not competitive; rather, it is designed to care for and collaborate with others external to itself. It is aware that others exist apart from itself and through empathy appreciates that they are also living beings. There is a clear sense of "I" and "not-I".

This caring for the other leads to the right hemisphere being intrinsically ethical: it will strive to do what is good for us all, not just what is good for itself; treating the other with kindness and compassion is a good strategy for the right hemisphere to achieve this. The right hemisphere wants to thrive, just as the left hemisphere does, and recognises that collaborating with others in a larger space than just itself is the way to do that.

Learning

Where the left hemisphere deals in transportable facts, procedures and the like, the right hemisphere develops a unique knowledge. New facts or information awaken existing neural networks and add to, and modify, them. As new information enters, our brain makes new connections.

When we learn many new things the networks that form can be so extensive that we "can't get our brains around it all". We have a sense that we know something, but we are not sure what it is.

The problem is that firing a neuron uses energy, so only a small proportion of neurons can fire simultaneously. As a large network begins to fire, we begin to sense that we know something; but since these early neurons must quieten down again for the remainder of the network to fire, we lose the sense of knowing. There's a saying: "neurons that fire together wire together". But when the neural network is too large, the neurons don't wire together fully, which means that we can't yet access the new knowledge.

To resolve this, the right hemisphere is able to compress neural networks. The brain keeps trying to find more efficient ways to make the same connections until the network is compact enough to fire together (and thus wire together) and we suddenly become aware of knowing something new. This new knowledge then becomes a building block or basis for further knowing. Anyone who has lived for any length of time will have a vast and unique knowledge of the world and how to act in it.

To summarise, the right hemisphere is always moving through a world that is new, and is open to information and events that are unfamiliar; it is better suited to identifying what might be a threat than the left hemisphere. However, it wants to live and enhance its life, and recognises that connecting with others is the best way to do this; accordingly, it is naturally empathic, caring, collaborative and ethical. The right hemisphere accumulates unique knowledge of the world and its worldview becomes increasingly sophisticated over time.

The hemispheres pay attention to the world in different ways

To be able to attend to the world in these different ways the two hemispheres call on different forms of attention. Three forms of attention activate the right hemisphere. At the highest level is *vigilance*, where the right hemisphere expects something unfamiliar, which might appear from anywhere; it's like a soldier on a castle parapet waiting for the first signs of an impending attack. *Alertness* is a level of attention a step down from vigilance. It's like a mother alert to the sounds of her baby sleeping in the room next door: she may not hear a dog bark but a slight whimper from her child will cause her to react, as would the sound of someone moving around – a potential threat to her child. Vigilance is a truly global form of attention: information will be detected from any direction and through any sense. Alertness is semi-global: new information will be detected if it relates to a given focus.

The third form of attention that the right hemisphere uses is *sustained attention*, which is directed towards an item, event or person and allows maximum awareness towards the object of attention. With sustained attention, the conscious mind is quiet, and attention is directed one hundred per cent to the object. When a person is the object of this attention, they feel really listened to; that they are valued. When someone feels like this they are likely to open their thinking and be willing to respond more thoughtfully. Using sustained attention leads to a greater sense of connection; this is not surprising, as we are engaging the right hemisphere, which can empathise and connect, and we are also encouraging the other person to engage their right hemisphere.

Focused attention is the only form of attention that the left hemisphere has access to. Quite literally focused, it uses visual input from a very small part of the centre of the eye, about one-and-a-half degrees around the axis, but not peripheral vision. This is perfect for threading a needle or other detailed work.

It should be apparent that each of these forms of attention has its natural role to play as we go about our lives. Focused attention is important when we do detailed work, exploiting and manipulating physical things or ideas that are familiar to us. The other forms of attention serve to connect us to the outside world (to people, things and new ideas), keeping us grounded, connected and up to date.

Recall that, as the left hemisphere receives new information, it temporarily suppresses our senses so that we stop paying attention to the source of this information and instead pay attention to ourselves. Because this tends to happen with familiar information, when we hear or see something that we think is familiar, we tend to miss a disproportionate amount of new information. The problem is that the right hemisphere cannot receive any new information either, while the senses are suppressed, so it cannot use new information to update its worldview. Furthermore, when we are not listening fully to someone, our connection with that person is reduced; when we miss things they've said, it's reduced even further.

The consequence of overusing focused attention is that we don't learn from our experiences; our worldview remains static and not representative of the real world. Overusing focused attention, we become transactional rather than relational with other people and we transact around things we are familiar with.

Our ability to handle familiar situations in automatic ways is incredibly valuable and has been a cornerstone of human progress; however, overspecialisation always has a downside. Missing new information or ideas in a complex environment can lead to poor decision making and stagnation. Encouraging the left hemisphere always to take the lead role means we lose the right hemisphere's ability to modulate the red brain, as the left hemisphere cannot control red brain triggering. So, although we can be very efficient, we can also be very fragile.

Schooling fosters left-hemisphere dominance and the red brain

Both of our brain hemispheres are important, and have different roles. They pay attention to the world in different ways – all of which are important for us to survive and thrive. However, our schooling encourages a disproportionate development of the left hemisphere and over-use of focused attention.

If we wanted to design a learning regime to favour the left hemisphere, then we would include lots of transportable knowledge to be memorised either consciously or by rote. We would dedicate a lot of time to detached, procedural repetition – mathematics being a good example of this. We would want to minimise interaction between students, so we would discourage it ("work quietly by yourselves") or prohibit it entirely by characterising it as "cheating". These measures would minimise engagement of the right hemisphere. We would keep lessons short and make no connections between different subject areas.

Because we practise using focused attention at school much more than the right-hemisphere forms (vigilance, alertness and sustained attention), the left hemisphere tends to become preferred. Let me emphasise that this favouring of the left hemisphere simply means that the left hemisphere is leading. Of course, the right hemisphere is being used as well; it is just not in the driving seat.

This makes learning languages difficult, for example. To become fluent in a foreign language, we use sustained attention – that is, the right hemisphere. Four-year-olds can learn languages effortlessly and fluently; yet it is a rare 18-year-old who can do the same: by 18, we automatically use focused attention for most things.

Another consequence of left-hemisphere preference is that it limits our control over the red brain, since the left hemisphere is unable to modulate the red brain. The left hemisphere–red brain combination leaves us individualistic and self-focused, competitive, often judgemental of others, particularly those who are not like us. We are resistant to change, literally not hearing information that does not fit into our worldview. This filtering of the new or different limits our ability to be creative.

The red brain makes us prone to anxiety, self-doubt, irrational dislike of others, and a sense of inferiority or superiority that has no rational basis. It encourages a fixed, rather than a growth, mindset. It can lead to sudden outbursts of rage. But we are controllable. Our thoughts stay within defined boundaries; and, as we approach these boundaries, our red brains trigger – we become anxious – and we retreat to what we are familiar with.

When I was young I was brought up as a Roman Catholic and, being very conscientious, I did everything I was told to do and believed everything I was told. Even in my twenties and thirties, if the thought arose in me to question the existence of God, my red brain would trigger and simply block the thought out; it was something my mind absolutely forbad me to contemplate. This prohibition on questioning the existence of God must have been drummed into me from a young age as I have no explicit memory of it.

I imagine the same thing occurs for many well-educated climate change deniers. Anything that would so challenge their worldview is simply blocked out; information that is present all around them is thus prevented from reaching the right hemisphere and contributing to their worldview.

So, we are conditioned at school to favour the use of focused attention and the left hemisphere. Since this prevents us from managing the red brain and, since we continue to favour the left hemisphere throughout school and beyond, our red brain is maintained through to adulthood.

We are constrained from developing higher consciousness

Our worldview evolves as we grow. Developmental psychologist Jean Piaget demonstrated that children move through different stages of mental development – of making sense of the world. If you show a five-year-old two glasses, one tall and thin, the other short and fat, and ask which one holds more water, they will say the taller one – even after watching you pour the same amount of water into each glass. At age five, we make sense of the world through our perceptions – we *are* our perceptions – and we perceive the taller glass to hold more. Adults find this cute and do not scold us for getting it wrong because this is how a five-year-old is supposed to be.

By age eight, practically every child will say the two glasses hold the same amount: at this age children *have* perceptions, but they are only one factor in the child's sense making; those perceptions no longer determine the child's response alone. The child's ability to make meaning has advanced considerably; and, again, we take this as being normal. In fact, we would be surprised if an eight-year-old were to give the five-year-old's response. By this stage, we expect them to be able to separate their perception from what they have learnt through observation.

Under normal conditions children move seamlessly through the different stages of meaning-making, with adults around them accommodating and supporting each level. Until recently it was believed that there was little further development of consciousness in adulthood. In the mid-1980s, however, Jane Loevinger discovered that there were multiple levels beyond childhood (summarised in the much-viewed 2005 *Harvard Business Review* article "Seven transformations of leadership" by David Rooke and Bill Torbert), but that few adults seemed to reach them.

Our left hemisphere's worldview is largely how we make sense of the world – it is our consciousness or awareness – and this allows many of our actions to be routine or automatic. It is the right hemisphere, with its more up-to-date worldview, that might give us a moment's pause: "Why, exactly, am I doing things like that?" We know that our left hemisphere's worldview is static – yet it's clear from our observation of children that there are shifts in consciousness. Each level is discrete; that is, shifts in meaning-making occur in a stepwise fashion just as the shift from being a five-year-old to being an eight-year-old is a step change.

Developing a new world view

In order for our consciousness to step up to the next level, our static worldview must dissolve and reform at a more sophisticated level. So what causes our static view to dissolve; and where does a new worldview come from?

The answer to the first question is straightforward: when faced with a challenge that we cannot make sense of in our current worldview, we are forced to find a new way. The research is clear that, at the early adult levels, something must upset our equilibrium: it's important that this matters to us so that we engage emotionally; and that it occurs in a supportive environment, so that we can let go of the world we know before we are clear about the world we are moving into.

The right hemisphere's view of the world is continuously developing as it takes in wide and varied new information from the world around it. Eventually, the gap between the static worldview held by the left hemisphere and the global view held by the right is so great that the static view starts to dissolve. The left hemisphere derives its new, more sophisticated worldview from the most up-to-date global view of the right. Once this is in place, the left hemisphere operates at a higher level of capability.

The disintegration of the old, static worldview leads to a period of disorientation as we lose a sense of worth in what we have done before, and are not sure what we need to do next. Our efficiency can drop, and we seem to go through a grieving process as things we once valued are lost. At this point we need support and acceptance to facilitate the shift, just as we naturally give to children. Clearly, our society is not set up to support adults in this way and, as we will see next, the focused attention–left hemisphere preference gets in the way of this process happening altogether.

What stops us moving up in consciousness?

The process of moving up a level in consciousness can be hindered by favouring the left hemisphere and its use of focused attention. We filter information coming in so that the global view does not develop very far from the static, local view; there is thus no pressure to change. The left hemisphere believes its worldview is the world. Full stop.

Our schooling encourages us to favour the left hemisphere and use focused attention and therefore constrains the normal, serial, stepwise development of adult consciousness.

One implication of constraining the stepwise development of consciousness in adults is that old people in modern societies are just that: old. In many earlier societies old people were "elders" who were valued members of their societies as they offered a level of wisdom and perspective; a level of consciousness and awareness that younger people had not developed.

A second implication is that eventually we get to a point where we force a change to take place, which explains the mid-life crisis that often leads to abrupt life changes in work or personal life (for example, career changes or divorce). This change can be traumatic because it is so long overdue.

A third, and very serious, implication is that, to cope with global problems such as human-induced climate change and resource depletion, we need many, many more people able to operate at higher levels of consciousness. Without this we will continue to operate from the same exploitative playbook, driven by low levels of awareness of the bigger picture.

The problem we now face

Just as nineteenth-century education reached its use-by date around the First World War, when having a population with little flexibility or adaptability became too limiting, so our current system is meeting its limits. Preferencing the left hemisphere and focused attention has made us very good at applying the knowledge accumulated by society to exploit the world around us; however, it has not prepared us to face a complex and ambiguous future.

We are facing problems now that human societies have never faced at this scale. Both climate change and resource depletion have occurred locally in the past, driving populations to move to more agreeable climates and where resources were more abundant. This has often led to societies themselves collapsing but humankind continuing to progress. We now face these challenges on a global scale: our agriculture is at risk, our industrial base is at risk and our societies' stability is at risk, all in ways that cannot be resolved locally.

Allowing the childhood mind to persist into adulthood, so that the two-mind state is normal, has produced a population that is capable and conforming, but which has limited ability to adapt to changing circumstances and adopt new ways of working. As we reach the limits of our current system, our anxiety levels rise, which exacerbates the problem, but also forces us towards change.

This is very serious. We are facing, for the first time in history, problems that require collaboration on a global scale. No country, no matter how large or powerful, can escape the effects of climate change by themselves. If we are to address and solve such problems then we need a critical mass of adults who can face up to such problems with courage, who can think creatively and collaborate with people who are different – culturally, socially, spiritually, politically; potentially in every way – and find solutions that work for the good of everyone.

There is no guarantee that we can do this, but it is certain that we cannot do it if we continue to develop adults who lack these quintessential twenty-first-century capabilities. Not only do we need people operating at higher levels of consciousness to face these complex problems, we also need people operating in the blue brain. Of course, these are linked: the more we operate in the blue brain, the more able we are to move up to higher levels of consciousness; moreover, the higher our level of consciousness, the easier it is to operate in the blue brain.

Chapter 5

How to get out of the red brain II – reduce triggering

THE RED BRAIN CAN BE triggered by a wide range of thoughts, memories, smells, visual cues and sounds that we have associated in the past with a negative experience. Some triggers can randomly appear in our thoughts; others need an external cue or prompt. In either case, the negative emotion that is awakened can cascade, causing the red brain to take over.

Random triggers can occur when a thought jumps into our mind while we are otherwise occupied – perhaps reading, watching the television, working or playing: we might suddenly realise we've forgotten something, recall a mistake that we recently made, or think of a challenging situation we will soon face. This thought can summon memories about what happened last time we forgot something, the consequences of that mistake, or what happened last time we faced this sort of challenge. These memories can set off our red brain.

The opposite of this situation is when we go into flow and have no distracting thoughts to snap us out again. Note that when we are in flow the red brain is absent. There is no hesitation in our actions, our minds are clear, and we think and move fluidly and intuitively.

As we noted in chapter 4, it takes about 15 minutes of continuous effort to go into flow, so each time we are distracted by a random thought, even when it does not trigger the red brain, we need another 15 minutes to get back into flow again. Without these intermittent interruptions we will stay longer in flow and be more productive. We become more competent in flow because, in this focused state, we refine our skills and establish new automatic responses or easier ways to get tasks done. Increasing our competence and productivity helps us feel good about ourselves and makes us more resilient to red brain triggering.

So to reduce the likelihood of our red brain triggering, we first look at ways to be in flow more often.

Using focused-attention meditation to stay in flow

We can improve our ability to remain in flow by not allowing internal distractions to get hold of our minds and divert our thoughts. People who largely operate in the left hemisphere and with an active red brain find it hard to go into flow, as their minds are easily distracted by thoughts that suddenly hold their attention – things they suddenly remember they need to do, or anxieties about what might happen if such-and-such doesn't go right. These uncontrolled and impulsive thoughts keep the red brain simmering if not actually fully triggered. So quietening them is a first step in reducing triggering. One way to do this is to use the most basic form of meditation.

There is no common, accepted definition of meditation; many practices exist, undoubtedly with different, and sometimes very profound, effects. The most basic form is known as focused-attention meditation. The idea is to focus on something – an object or, often, your breathing – and, when you notice that you have been distracted by a thought, to gently let the thought go and return your focus to the object or your breath. Over time, this practice increases our ability to focus, so we become less distracted by thoughts that might trigger the red brain.

In principle, meditation is relatively simple and can be done anywhere, more-or-less, by anyone. No equipment or special clothing is needed. The meditator begins by taking up a comfortable physical posture, neither too tense nor too relaxed. This can be sitting in a chair or lying on a bed.

Strong scientific evidence has demonstrated the benefits of focused-attention meditation, which aims to calm and centre the mind in the present moment while developing the capacity to remain alert to, and reduce the power of, distractions.

Meditation enables maladaptive memories to arise without us putting them into action. We allow these thoughts to arise (a sudden anxiety about something we have not done, or a pang of guilt about the way we spoke to our partner, for example) and, when we notice that we have become distracted, then, without beating ourselves up in any way, we bring our focus back to our breath or the object we are using to hold our attention. This process begins to reduce the number of random memories (and associated negative feelings – anxiety or guilt, for example) that appear unprompted in our minds.

Limitations of focused-attention meditation

Meditation originates in the Hindu tradition and was disseminated via Buddhism to a wider audience. For three thousand years, India has been a caste-based society, hierarchical to the extreme; it thus discourages full adult development, instead perpetuating a culture where the red brain remains active.

In this context, meditation is an effective means for controlling or managing the red brain in that it reduces our internal triggers and helps us to stay in flow. However, it does not disturb the status quo. Indeed, meditation has been widely supported in many societies: it helps improve performance – people are more productive and calmer – but it does not threaten the basic set up of left hemisphere leading and the two-mind state.

A further limitation of meditation is that it is largely a solitary activity, which is generally not practical to do for more than an hour or so per day, and probably much less. Those who can meditate for many hours a day (monks, for example) may see further benefits, but these are not readily accessible to most people.

Meditation, therefore (or contemplative prayer in other traditions), is a method for self-management of the red brain, but it will not cause the red brain to fade away. If we aim to remove the red brain altogether, meditation is a necessary first practice to improve focus, particularly in situations where we are alone. Waking in the middle of the night with your mind racing is a perfect opportunity to practise this form of meditation. Similarly, if you find your heart racing as you are about to speak in public, a few moments of focused-attention meditation can be very helpful. Regular practice reduces the random intrusion of red brain triggers.

Using mindfulness to control red brain triggering

Quietening random thoughts is an important first step in controlling red brain triggering; the next step is to be able to resist red-brain triggering whether the stimulus is internal or external.

Mindfulness is a second form of meditation that activates the right hemisphere through using particular forms of attention. Since the right hemisphere can modulate the red brain, by training the mind to operate more often with the right hemisphere as first responder, we can avoid red brain triggering far more successfully and face the world more calmly.

With the left hemisphere in first-responder mode, a red brain trigger cannot be stopped when it occurs. With the right hemisphere in this mode we have the potential to dial down the negative emotion as it begins to well up inside of us, and so return to equilibrium. We can control red brain triggering.

The practice is usually described as awareness mindfulness or open mindfulness. Like focused-attention meditation, mindfulness is a simple practice. We can practise it as we might meditation, sitting or lying down; however, we can also practise mindfulness as we are doing something else such as eating, walking the dog or driving. This means that we can practise mindfulness for more time in a day than we can practise focused-attention meditation.

At its most basic, mindfulness is being aware of what is happening inside our bodies. For example, through paying attention to each part of our bodies in turn, we identify sensations or feelings and just stay with them for a few moments before moving on to the next part. Mindfulness is also being aware of what is happening around us, for example, observing the trees, bushes, flowers as we walk through the park. It includes combining the inner and the outer: What are the sensations in my legs as I walk through the park? Eating is another way to combine inner and outer: we can notice the look, smell and texture of a mouthful of toast, the sensations in our mouth and on our tongue, the feelings in our throat as we swallow, the rising fullness in our stomachs.

Because the right hemisphere is deeply connected into the body, we can only be in the moment and focus on bodily sensations through activating the right hemisphere and its way of paying attention to the world. For anyone who has learned to favour their left hemisphere and has an active red brain, this begins to rebalance the two hemispheres and accustoms the brain to rely less on the left hemisphere.

On the path to removing the red brain, mindfulness can be very helpful, so take any opportunity when you are alone and active to be mindful. As you travel to work, rather than letting your thoughts wander, bring your attention to the moment, to what is around you – the smells, the sights. Bring your attention into your body: what sensations do you feel? Become aware of different parts of the body in turn. All these practices help to activate the right hemisphere and get it used to being in control.

Mindfulness practice is becoming increasingly popular as levels of anxiety in society rise and the left hemisphere–

red brain combination becomes untenable. The welfare state has, since the Second World War, largely been able to keep the left hemisphere–red brain combination viable: if people just did as they were supposed to, they would be supported through unemployment benefit, pensions and affordable health care. However, the welfare state is breaking down and this support is becoming visibly reduced. Now there is too much uncertainty; too much that will trigger red brains on a regular basis.

The science indicates that mindfulness is very beneficial in reducing depression and anxiety and improving wellbeing in general. It also improves our ability to engage with other people.

Using mindfulness to extinguish red brain triggers

Reducing random triggering of the red brain and managing triggering by encouraging the right hemisphere to be first responder are both key steps in reducing triggering events, but it is by systematically removing many of the triggers themselves that even more progress can be made.

As we have seen, mindfulness is a very powerful practice in bringing red brain triggering under conscious control. Yet it has another, perhaps even more powerful, effect. Through mindfulness practice the brain can pull up a memory and extinguish the associated negative emotion, replacing it with a neutral or positive emotion. What this means is that we can gradually extinguish the events that trigger the red brain. A certain person triggers the red brain each time we see them. Using mindfulness we can get to the point where we can see this person and no red brain triggering occurs. Through the systematic practice of mindfulness, we can increase the range of circumstances in which we can stay operating in the blue brain.

Neuroplasticity is the concept that our brain can change by how we use it, and that our brains remain plastic in this way our whole lives. For example: a violinist will see thickening of the brain areas that control her fingers as she practises; stroke patients have been able to rebuild brain tissue by manipulating their limbs such that, over time, they can regain at least partial control over limbs that became paralysed when the stroke damaged their brain.

Focused-attention meditation and mindfulness are powerful ways to change our brains. Mindfulness thickens and develops areas of the brain that increase our self-awareness, self-regulation and self-transcendence. This means we improve our capacity for awareness within and around us; we are able to choose our response to a stimulus rather than responding in an automatic way; and we can get beyond a focus on ourselves alone and recognise, and empathise with, others. These are all characteristics of the blue brain.

Together these three capacities – staying in flow, controlling red brain triggering and extinguishing red brain triggers – enable us to be self-determining: to be aware of what is happening around us, to be alert to other people and then choose what action we will take. This action is not compliance, driven by an internal "should"; nor is it defiance, driven by a desire *not* to follow a rule or regulation; but, rather, it is a free choice based on what is best for me and for others, given these circumstances. It is a creative response.

How to practise

To extinguish red brain triggers using mindfulness, we put ourselves in the presence of a red brain trigger, allow the emotion to begin welling up, and then focus on the sensations we are having and let the feelings subside again. In order to focus on an internal sensation, we must engage the right hemisphere, which enables us to wind back the red brain.

A powerful way to do this is in relation to a colleague or other co-worker who, for whatever reason, triggers our red brain. Remember, seeing or being with this person may trigger memories for the most banal of reasons: they have a similar jaw shape to someone who bullied us when we were eight years old; they have a way of speaking or behaving that we do not like in ourselves; or they represent an authority figure and that is enough to trigger our red brain.

To extinguish these triggers, we could view this person from a distance and mindfully allow the triggering to begin and then quieten down again. It may take four to six weeks of practising for all the triggers associated with this person to be extinguished but, when they are, we will be able to remain in the blue brain in their presence.

By following this practice systematically, over time, we can gradually extinguish triggers that affect our day-to-day performance. There will still be triggers that we see only rarely, which we will need to deal with and then extinguish as they arise. Obviously, over time, these will become fewer and fewer.

In this chapter we have learned how focused-attention meditation can help us to reduce and even eliminate random thoughts and potential red brain triggers from popping unprompted into our minds. The practice of mindfulness goes further, allowing us to resist red brain triggering and to increase our control when it does.

Using mindfulness in the presence of red brain triggers allows our brains to extinguish the negative feelings associated with memories and replace them with neutral or positive feelings. Over time, we can eliminate a wide range of day-to-day red brain triggers, leaving only the less frequent ones for further work.

Yet, despite the power of meditation and mindfulness, neither can cause the red brain to fade away altogether. Using these practices increases our control enormously, but we still have a red brain that can trigger in moments of great stress or illness.

We need a further practice to cause the red brain to fade away altogether, which we will learn about in chapter 8.

Chapter 6
Strengthening the blue brain

WE HAVE FOCUSED SO FAR on the red brain: what it is, where it comes from, how to get out of it, how to reduce it triggering in the first place and, as we'll see in chapter 8, how to remove it all together. We have not focused much at all on the blue brain and how we can strengthen it. Strengthening the blue brain has two purposes: one is to make us more resistant to red brain triggering; the second and, in the end, more important reason is to help us to be at our very best more of the time.

I would like to share two stories about seeing teachers operate in the blue brain and the effect this had on me. The first of these was some years ago in the UK. The principal of the school was very excited about one of her teachers, and she asked me to come and observe this teacher in class. It was a joy to see the technical skill of this teacher: how she included absolutely everybody in the class; how she gently challenged the thinking of each child; how she posed questions, then follow-up questions, such that every child in this relatively young class was thinking deeply; the children gave thoughtful responses and, clearly, every one of them was engaged in the lesson.

But the effect on me was also very interesting. I had the same overriding feeling as the children: I wanted this experience to continue; it was hard to leave the classroom. I recognised that I was in the presence of somebody operating fully in the blue brain and the effect was to lift me up into the blue brain as well. This prompted me to wonder for the first time how we could do this ourselves, without relying on somebody else to do it for us.

So that was my first example of seeing an outstanding teacher in action. The second one occurred in Adelaide much more recently. I was engaged in a program called "instructional rounds", where small groups spend ten or fifteen minutes observing several different classes to gather evidence around current practice. In one class, the teacher was relatively new to teaching and to this school, and the principal did not know her very well.

Again, the class was an absolute joy to behold. These were older children, perhaps year eight, and a class discussion was taking place. It was beautifully organised by the teacher, who was clearly operating in the blue brain: her full attention was out to the students. Very little of the discussion went through the teacher: most passed from student to student. The students were thoughtful before responding and everyone was taking part. There was nobody looking out of the window or sitting quietly in a corner; every student was fully engaged. Again, my overriding feeling was that I wanted it to continue; I wanted this experience of being held in the blue brain to go on.

Being in the blue brain

Operating in the blue brain we are really at our best. We move into, or are held in, the blue brain when we feel safe and in control: typically, this is when we feel unconditionally loved or respected, when we feel valued, when we feel listened to, when we have clarity over what to do, and when permission is asked of us (so we have some control), when we are acknowledged and included, when people are generous to us, when people make themselves vulnerable to us.

A lot of things that bring us into the blue brain are the actions, the attitudes and the mind states of people around us. In the two classes I visited, it was the mind state of the teacher that raised the children – and the observers – into the blue brain. What is happening around us affects our brain state – particularly the people around us. We are social beings.

When we move into the blue brain, we exhibit three distinct characteristics: we are confident; we are collaborative; and we are creative.

Our confidence is related to the underlying need that we have for competence. When we are competent at something, we develop confidence in what we can do. We think more about success than failure; and we want to keep moving forward.

Collaboration reflects our underlying need for connection. We need to be connected to ourselves and to others; we need to be grounded and we need a sense of purpose – to be connected to something larger than ourselves. We saw in the classroom stories how another human can affect our mind state.

In the blue brain, we instinctively engage with other people. We have the desire to get people together, and think about who can help us, who could work with us in some way. We have greater empathy for those around us.

Creativity relates to our underlying need for self-determination – to decide for ourselves what to do. As we strengthen our ability to think and act for ourselves, we have an urge to create something new – new for us, and perhaps new for others as well. There is an excitement about the possibilities that could arise.

When we go into the blue brain, we have those three characteristics or drives available to us. How do we strengthen those over time?

How to strengthen the blue brain

Strengthening the blue brain is a bit like renovating a house. We're not only making it more attractive and functional, but also more able to stand up to winter storms. We want to build capabilities that will allow us to weather red brain triggering that might take place in the future.

There are nine strategies we can follow. We start by reinforcing our sense of confidence, our sense of collaboration and our sense of creativity, bedding those feelings down so they become solid and persistent – feelings that we can rely upon.

Then we enhance these feelings by modifying how we think or act so that operating in the blue brain is more who we are than simply being a temporary mind state.

Finally, we transform the way we think and act so that operating in the blue brain becomes an external way of being rather than an internal mind state.

Reinforcing what we have

Accept your confidence

Reinforcing our confidence is like putting extra guy ropes on a tent so that it can better weather the storm ahead. We reinforce our confidence by accepting it.

When I feel confident, or competent about something, I reflect on my strengths and accomplishments to establish my confidence as being part of a pattern. I am confident, not just because something has gone well; I am confident because I have strengths; I have a history of accomplishments and together these justify my confidence. I accept my right to be confident because I am good at what I do. I am competent, and the confidence is justified.

Next, I express gratitude for the success and opportunities that I have had. The more I express gratitude for something, the more I will increase my belief that this is genuine for me. This was not chance; this was not somebody else's effort. I have done something, I am confident in what I have done, I am competent in my actions and I am acknowledging that fact by being grateful.

Finally I visualise that the future may be better still. I am competent today; I am confident today; and, if I see myself continuing like this, I will become more competent and will have the confidence to act successfully in the future.

To reinforce my confident feelings, I can reflect on my strengths and accomplishments, express gratitude for successes and the opportunities that I have had, and visualise that the future can be better still. Each of these actions is putting my confidence into a solid framework, making it stronger and more resilient.

Be discerning

A hot air balloon is only useful when it is up in the air. To keep it up in the air, we have to keep providing hot air to it. In the same way, we reinforce our desire for collaboration by continuing to connect with people. But we want to engage with people where the conversation is positive and useful, so we need to be discerning. Avoid comparison and rumination, as these can deflate our balloon. Either leave those conversations, or change the subject.

Seek out those who respond collaboratively, who respond in the way that we ourselves would like to respond, so that we reinforce the blue brain within each of us. This leads naturally to listening fully to the other person – a key support – and responding with kindness and compassion in ways that are helpful. Ask questions that illuminate a better future, rather than those that dwell on the past. As we both move deeper into the blue brain, then our ability to be collaborative deepens also.

To summarise, we can reinforce our capacity for collaboration by avoiding conversations that are not helpful, seeking out those who are open to collaboration and striving as much as we can to have solutions-focused, forward-looking conversations.

Engage with creative ideas

We strengthen our creativity through engaging with the world around us and the ideas of others. Reading is one of the easiest ways to do this, but we can likewise involve ourselves through film, art and music. By engaging in the creativity of others, we reinforce our own.

Being creative does not mean we have to keep coming up with good ideas. It's hard to read even a fraction of the books published each year – roughly 300,000 in the US and 30,000 in Australia. However, we can access summaries of books and, in a matter of minutes, grasp the essence of the ideas that are proposed. Regular exposure to creative ideas – even a few minutes each day – helps to reinforce our creativity.

We can read widely to participate in the creativity of others. In the first instance, read as a student: that is, read to learn what you can from what others are thinking or feeling. It is important to refrain from judging or comparing as you read. Allow what is being discussed to enter fully into your mind without either of these filters. You want to participate in the ideas, not shoot them down or close them out. Regularly reflect on the reading to allow new learnings to emerge. Clearly, you can follow this same process with art, theatre, music and film in the same way, although reading is probably the most accessible thing for people in busy times.

When I started the journey that I am still on now, I was recommended a book by theologian and philosopher Paul Tillich, called *The courage to be*. I think I have read that book 18 times over the years. The first time I read it I could only fully grasp the first chapter. I kept reading and rereading, participating in the creativity that Tillich brought to his thinking until gradually I could replicate some of his arguments and discussions more fully in my mind, which led me to being far more creative in my own work.

We have now looked at the first set of strategies for strengthening the blue brain: reinforce our confidence; be discerning about who we engage with so we maintain our sense of collaboration; and engage with the creativity of others.

Building capacity

Embrace your confidence

Having accepted our confidence, the next step is to embrace it. This is like having a concrete pillar to hold on to when the wind is blowing. We have reinforced our confidence, we have put it into a framework that is grounded in who we are and now we are going to embrace it: "Yes, this is something solid. No matter what happens I remain confident that I can weather it."

To embrace our confidence, we allow it to define us: the confidence I have is solid and real and I can always have it. My capabilities do not depend upon transitory feelings. If my red brain triggers and I feel down, I need to keep in mind that I am no less competent; this feeling of being down does not define me – it is just a feeling, which is transitory. In minutes or hours or days I will feel fully confident again because it is *that* which defines me. Some of the strategies discussed in chapter 2 – for example, evaluating ruminating thoughts and relabelling your feelings – are useful here.

Setbacks then become a way to get better, rather than being deflating or inducing guilt. By embracing our confidence and the underlying competence that supports it, we know we can get through anything. When something does go wrong, we know we are competent enough to handle it and so we are not fazed by it. We stay in the blue brain despite the challenges.

Some years ago, I was feeling anxious about a major presentation I was about to make when I suddenly thought: I am going to be the best that I can be today, given all the circumstances. If, after I finish, I think, "if only I had done it that way", that means that I have learnt; next time I *will* do it that way and my presentation will be better still. From that point on, I have never felt guilty about screwing up because I never intended to screw up. I was the best I could be at the time; what followed was simply a great source of learning. We can only ever be as good as we can be and, when we operate in the blue brain, we learn.

Include more people

We enhance our collaborative capacity by connecting with more people. We now want to engage with people we would not typically engage with, seeking out conversations with people whom we otherwise might avoid. To move past our first impressions, we want to listen to them with full attention and respond with kindness. In so doing, we become better at collaborating with people with whom we would not, or could not, normally be collaborative.

You might initially assume that a person you meet at a party is boring; but pay full attention to that person, listening to them to get beyond your first impression and, in a couple of minutes you will find interesting things about them and become more engaged in the connection. Because they are different from you, this activity strengthens your capacity to be collaborative. We can enhance our collaboration by including others whom we might not normally include.

Share others' ideas

A way to enhance our own creativity is to begin articulating the ideas of others as we study them. So far, we have engaged with the creativity of others by reading (or watching or listening) as a student; now we can begin to read as a teacher. As you read (or look at film or art), imagine how you might share the ideas with another person. How would you teach this material? Periodically articulate the view that is presented to you. Pause, and in your own mind, express it as a full idea, then share these thoughts with others. We enhance our creativity by sharing the creative ideas of others with those around us.

Transforming ourselves and others

The final set of strategies for strengthening our blue brain is about transformation: we can turn our capabilities into something else.

Serve others

We can transform our reinforced and enhanced confidence by turning it into service. When we are fully confident about our own abilities, we can focus our attention outwards onto the needs of others. Moreover, when we have no doubts about our own competence, we can detach ourselves from the outcome. The teachers I described earlier in this chapter were completely in the service of the children:

completely at ease, entirely confident in their own abilities. They transformed that confidence into service.

To do so, start by focusing on the needs of others, rather than investing in a particular outcome. In this space you will no longer feel the need to convince people of your point of view. Still present your point of view, of course, but if it does not serve them, that is fine. The conversation can move on to something that may be of greater service. This is particularly powerful for salespeople: often we try to sell something and are disappointed when we fail. Being in service, we are focused on the person's needs and, once they believe that we understand their problem as well as, or even better than they do (as we should if we are providing a solution), they will want to buy from us; we no longer need to "sell".

With this mindset, no longer have you "failed" when something you are trying to do does not work. Rather, whatever outcome occurred is the best outcome that was possible in these circumstances and with your current abilities. To transform your confidence into service, first detach yourself from the outcome; then identify, and offer, your very best contribution.

When you are on the receiving end of someone being in service, as I was in those two classes, there is a tremendous feeling of being in the blue brain. You want this level of service. You want the attention of this person. You want it to continue.

Enable others

We can transform our collaboration by enabling other people. This is like having a superpower where people develop just because you are there. The teachers I described earlier facilitated a connection between every child and the observers and brought everybody up into the blue brain. They were enabling all of us to be at our best by simply being there.

To do this we must listen with full attention to everyone we meet – no matter who, or where. It means listening without judgement or comparison. We do not judge what they are saying. We do not think, "Well, that happened to me too", or, "That happened to so-and-so", or, "That's just like ...". We avoid doing anything in our conscious mind that gets in the way of paying full attention to the other person; we do not pull up any memories.

Whatever the other person says or does, we respond with kindness and compassion. They may be angry or defensive, arrogant or sulky; they may say hurtful things. We respond always with kindness – a desire for their happiness, or with compassion – a desire to reduce their suffering.

Listening like this is powerful: we transform our ability to collaborate into something that enables another person to be at their best. The way we engage with them lifts them up into the blue brain.

Contribute ideas

We have reinforced our creativity through reading widely, participating in the ideas of others without judging them. We have then enhanced our creativity by replicating those ideas and working out how to teach them. To transform our creativity, we contribute our own ideas, building on the ideas of others. As Newton wrote: "If I have seen a little further it is by standing on the shoulders of giants."

We first read as a student and then as a teacher; we now want to read as a thought leader – to read with a sense of, "What do I really think about this?" Now as you read, you consider what you really think; you might think: Yes, I agree with that, *and* it relates to *x*, which this author has not mentioned. Or you might disagree: This is no longer correct; this book is ten years old and the world has moved on.

I learned a very effective way to do this from Matt Church, founder of Thought Leaders, which involves two notepads. One is a "yes, and" notepad and the other is a "no, but" notepad. As you read, quite systematically write, "Yes, I agree with that and I would I add this to it" or, "No, I disagree with that but here is an alternative possibility".

As you read somebody else's ideas, you create a set of new ideas: the notes you take represent a set of ideas unique to you. In publishing those ideas to a wider audience, you add to a body of knowledge, expanding what is already known. You are creating new content, new thoughts, which can be shared with a wider audience simply by publishing through a blog or email list. You are now being creative in your own right; you are making your own unique contribution.

This is thought leadership. To begin with, you participate in creativity as a student; then, as a teacher; and, finally, as a thought leader. You are creating new ideas beyond what existed before. The capacity to do this strengthens your ability to stay in the blue brain considerably. Every time you read, you use brain functions only available in the advanced parts of the brain. The more you practise, the more habitual this becomes.

	Confidence	Collaboration	Creativity
Reinforce	Accept	Discern	Engage
Enhance	Embrace	Include	Share
Transform	Serve	Enable	Contribute

Nine strategies for reinforcing the blue brain

These are the nine strategies we can use when in the blue brain, to help us return to the blue brain, and to strengthen our blue brain. Ideally, we want to reach the transformation stage where our confidence becomes service, our collaboration enables others to be at their best and our creativity contributes to knowledge.

Chapter 7
How we can avoid creating a red brain in our children

WE LEARNED IN CHAPTERS 3 AND 4 that a red brain develops in childhood. It is an inadvertent consequence of adults' seemingly normal efforts to control children's behaviour – most by imposing rules, regulations and values and subsequently enforcing them through rewards and punishments.

The key word is "imposing". Imposition creates within the child's memory a whole range of "shoulds" and "musts", along with anxieties, and memories of how bad they felt when things went wrong. This shadow of the childhood mind persists into adulthood so that, when these memories are triggered, the childhood mind fires up again and the red brain takes control.

Managing children's behaviour

In any family, school, or community, children are expected to adopt behavioural norms in order to fit in. To help children fit in, we often attempt to control them by imposing – and enforcing – rules about how children should behave. This imposition frequently means that the child behaves in ways desired by others rather than behaving in ways towards which it is internally driven for its own current wellbeing.

When rules are imposed a child can respond in three ways. They can comply – following the rules but not internalising them and, if enforcement drops off, then so will compliance. They can half-heartedly accept – sometimes observing the rules and sometimes not. Or they can resist. Although following these rules and behaviours is necessary to function fully, in none of these cases does the child internalise and integrate them into their own way of being.

A compliant child is seen as being a good boy or girl. If the child resists, punishment or coercion is often used to elicit the desired behaviour. In the case of half-hearted acceptance, an inducement or reward is often proposed.

However they respond, the child forgoes the opportunity for self-determination; the rule determines their behaviour, not their own volition. Being able to self-regulate is a key internal drive towards proper adult development; reduced self-determination will lead to anxiety and difficulty in adapting to social conditions; it will lead to red brain behaviours.

However, imposing rules is not the only way to obtain the desired behaviour. Children integrate rules when they can determine for themselves the value of behaving in a certain way, which means that they continue to do so even when there is no external imposition. They have fully internalised the new behaviour. A simple example is an adolescent emptying rubbish bins around the house: if the chore is seen as an imposition, a compliant adolescent will empty the bins when reminded to. However, when the behaviour is fully integrated, the adolescent will take on the responsibility of emptying the bins – they regard it as important – and will monitor the bins to empty them as needed.

When my own children were very young, perhaps five or six, they would come out when I was working in the garden and want to help. I would try to direct them to do this or that and, after a short while they would lose interest and wander away. I remember vividly thinking that it was a lost opportunity but, at the time, I simply didn't know what to do: I didn't think of trying to understand what motivated them, or finding them something that *they* would feel was worthwhile to do. Needless to say, they soon stopped offering their help.

In retrospect, I realise that I was too focused on completing the task I had started; I had learned at school that this was how successful adults behaved. When my daughters came out to help, I did not recognise the opportunity to be a father and support their development (and create long-term helpers in the process); instead I continued to focus on the task. I could easily have taken ten minutes out, sat down with them and asked what they felt like doing to help, and then supporting them in that. Of course, their work would probably not have helped me complete the overall task, but that is not the point: they would have been doing something that they had felt would help me, and I would have showed that I valued their help. Over time their contribution would have increased and coming out to help would be a natural part of who they were becoming.

In one study at the University of Rochester, researchers assessed the extent to which elementary-school children were motivated to do their schoolwork, comparing groups where regulations were imposed and where regulations were more integrated. They asked the teachers of these students to rate how motivated each student was, and they asked the children themselves how hard they tried in school.

Teachers considered students with high levels of imposed regulation, and students with high levels of self-regulation to be very motivated; and, in both cases, the children themselves reported that they were trying hard to do well. But similarities finished there. Those students working with imposed regulation were extremely anxious about school and did not appear to cope well with failure, whereas the more self-regulating students enjoyed school and demonstrated patterns of coping when things went wrong. Memories associated with anxieties and coping behaviours will form red brain triggers later in life. The self-regulating child will have far fewer of these.

Children will integrate rules or norms of behaviour – that is, regulate themselves – if they are supported to be self-determining. In the case of emptying the bins, you might have a discussion around all the chores that need to be done by everyone in the household and allow the adolescent to choose which ones they will accept responsibility for doing.

Similarly, supporting the young child in an activity that they find meaning in, and that they see as being helpful, develops self-regulation. This may take longer, initially, but time is saved in the long-run by not having to chase up chores that have not been done, or not done well, and by having children who are happy to help when they see their parents doing something.

THREE DRIVES THAT SHAPE BEHAVIOUR

We are driven to meet our physical needs, to seek pleasure and avoid pain, and to be our best selves. These three drivers motivate us to act in particular ways and people have – to a greater or lesser extent – used them to control others.

The most basic is the drive to meet our physical needs. We seek food when we are hungry and water when we are thirsty. We seek affection, especially when young, so that we can grow confidently and healthily. As we mature we have a drive towards sexual reproduction to pass our genes onto future generations. These are all normal and healthy drives that we share with many other living things. Exploiting these drives to control behaviour is simply not sustainable. Yes, we can starve people, but we also damage their ability to be productive, to do work. We can starve children of affection, but this also can cause significant mental damage, reducing the ability to do work. Exploiting this drive is not effective if our aim is to get people to work longer and harder than they might choose to do.

Our drive to seek pleasure and avoid pain has been manipulated most effectively to control us. When we have a choice, our preference is towards something that makes us feel good – the honey in the bee hive – and away from what gives us pain – the stings from angry bees. Controlled motivation, or use of rewards and punishment to exploit this drive, suits simple work that can be easily sequenced into steps; however, it reduces our ability to do complex work. For most of human history this has not been a constraint.

It is controlled motivation – reward and punishment – that creates the red brain as a child grows into adulthood. When it is externally imposed upon the growing brain, controlled motivation distorts its development. Ranging from violent physical punishment at one end of the spectrum to the offer of conditional love and affection (if the child does as they are told) at the other, controlled motivation gets us to do more of the work that somebody wants from us than we would otherwise freely choose to do. But it comes at a cost.

Simply complying with an imposed set of rules is no longer a viable way to succeed in life, where work is increasingly complex and demands creativity, collaboration and confidence. As we have seen, it is possible for the red brain to fade away, but this takes considerable effort. It would be much easier not to create the red brain in the first place.

Autonomous motivation is the internal drive to grow towards our best selves. It has only been recognised as a form of motivation since the late 1960s (its original proposal having been dismissed in the late 1940s). When this form of motivation is supported – and controlled motivation is absent – the child has the best chance of developing into a healthy adult, operating fully in the blue brain.

Every parent and every educator wants their children to become well-integrated and successful members of a healthy society: in other words, adults who operate in the blue brain all the time. It is more important than ever that our children grow up this way. For this to happen, we need to support children's autonomous motivation.

Supporting our children's healthy growth

How do we avoid creating a red brain in our children?

The short answer is that we respond to a child's behaviour with the clear understanding that he or she is a child. In the same way that we allow for children's unsophisticated understanding of the world because they are still developing mentally, we accept that they will say and do things that are inappropriate. But that's OK: they are children.

In effect, we are responding to the child in the blue brain: no matter what the child says or does, we respond with kindness. Most of us find it difficult to respond in this way with adults, since they trigger our red brains much more readily; but it is more achievable with children, especially our own children. It is easier to do this when we understand that children are autonomously motivated to become their best selves, if we just create the space.

There is a great deal of research that shows – for people of all ages – we are innately driven to become our best selves through becoming more competent, more self-determining and more connected. These internal drives, if satisfied, allow us to live well. They allow a child to grow up in a healthy, well-adjusted way.

Being competent means that we can act effectively in the world: using our knowledge and skills, and engaging with others. Children are driven to gain knowledge, develop skills, and to understand and fit in with socially acceptable norms of behaviour. Kindergartens, preschools, schools and a range of extracurricular activities – chess, swimming, football clubs, for example – provide the opportunity for children to build competence, as well as in the home.

Being self-determining, we can face up to a situation and not be controlled by it. We are not compliant – allowing the situation to control us; nor are we defiant. We can build this capability in our children through refraining from the use of controlled motivation – reward and punishment – and supporting the development of autonomous motivation where a child does something because it is enjoyable or interesting.

What if something is not enjoyable or interesting, but the child still needs to do it (for their healthy development)? In these cases, a child will do something that is challenging or boring if it connects to something that they value (to be a swimming star they need to train every day) or, importantly, they don't want to let someone down by not doing their best – being strongly connected to a parent or teacher, for example.

We can meet our child's need for connection – and support their autonomous motivation – by loving them unconditionally. If this need is not met, a child may become needy, behaving in ways that are not necessarily in the child's best interest. In loving a child unconditionally, we do not make our regard for them conditional on what they say or do. Yes, there are consequences for inappropriate behaviours, but our regard for them is not diminished.

If you want to train a puppy, use controlled motivation. If you want to educate a child, controlled motivation should play no role at all.

What stops us supporting autonomy

The most important thing we can do to help a child grow up free of a red brain is to support their autonomous development. However, various things can prevent adults from supporting children to be self-determining. An adult with a controlling personality may find that any challenge to their authority triggers their red brain, so that children learn to be compliant – or else. Alternatively, an adult may want to be supportive but lacks the skills to be so. Or they might believe it is important but have other pressures that take precedence.

The environment itself can make it difficult to support autonomy in children. Repeatedly, educators recount that they came into teaching eager and excited to work with students, to help them develop both academically and personally, but over time, as the pressures and demands have intensified, they have lost much of their initial enthusiasm.

Educators point to an ever-fuller curriculum – which they are obliged to cover even when their instincts tell them that some things are just not useful or helpful – and to the pressures on them to get high standardised test scores across their classes. These types of pressures often cause teachers to become more controlling: they feel pressured, so they, in turn, pressure their students.

In his book *Why we do what we do*, Edward L Deci describes an experiment that demonstrates how pressure to produce high-performing students causes teachers to become more controlling. Two groups of teachers were asked to teach students to solve problems. The teachers were given plenty of time to practise with the problems, and had both a list of useful hints and the actual solutions to all the problems. The teachers were randomly assigned to one of two groups, and everything was the same for the two groups except for one additional statement given to the teachers in one group: "Remember, it is your responsibility as a teacher to make sure your students perform up to high standards."

The sessions were recorded and then analysed. Teachers who had been reminded about their students' performance spent twice as much time talking during the teaching session as the other teachers, made three times as many directives, and made three times as many controlling statements (e.g. using words like "should" and "must"). As Deci says, "It is all quite ironic. Parents, politicians, and school administrators all want students to be creative problem-solvers and to learn material at a deep, conceptual level. But in their eagerness to achieve these ends, they pressure teachers to produce. The paradox is that the more they do that, the more controlling the teachers become, which, as we have seen so many times, undermines intrinsic motivation, creativity, and conceptual understanding in the students."

The harder the teachers are pushed to get results, the less likely it is that the important results will be achieved and the more we are creating the conditions for the red brain to exist in adulthood.

Although the experiment was done with teachers, it is relevant to anyone in a position of authority. When parents or leaders feel more pressured, it is also more difficult for them to support the development of self-determination of children or staff. We have learned to respond to stress by controlling others: our red brain triggers and our focus shifts to our own needs; away from the needs of those in our care or under our responsibility.

What this means for the longer term is that people in such positions – teachers, parents, leaders – will not be very effective in supporting the self-determination of their students, children and employees if they do not have their own support; support that shields them from unnecessary pressures.

But people don't want to be self-determining!

School leaders often say to me that one of their great problems in developing twenty-first-century skills (which need the blue brain) in their students is that students just do not want to be self-determining and demand to be told what to do.

Indeed, if you control people enough, they will typically begin to act as if they want to be controlled. This is a self-protective strategy: they become outwardly focused, looking for clues about what those in authority expect of them; looking for what will keep them out of trouble. In a school context, the clear message is that teachers want students to do well in high-stakes tests so students, in this state of mind, want to know what they have to do to achieve that.

To some extent, people adapt to being controlled and act as if they do not want the very thing that is integral to their nature – namely, the opportunity to be self-determining. They probably fear that they will be judged – perhaps even punished – if they make the wrong choice. However, sometimes when teachers or parents say that children do not want choice, they are justifying – even if subconsciously – their own controlling behaviour (behaviour that developed because *their* teachers or parents had not supported development of their own self-determination).

When people in positions of authority are controlling, they actively prevent others – those they are supposed to help – from developing autonomy. Today this is counter-productive, but it was baked into the cake fifty years ago when self-determination was not a desired education outcome; at least, not for the masses.

What all this means is that being supportive of self-determination can be very difficult, especially with people who have become accustomed to being controlled. We must be patient and work with children (and adults) to reawaken what is basic to their nature and what will always (in the long run) lead to more positive results.

How to awaken self-determination

We need to help people get back to the place where they are vital, interested, and eager to take on challenges and responsibilities. We need to promote their self-determination; in part, by providing them with choice – and, critically, with unconditional support of the choices they make. This unconditional support allows people to try and to fail, where failure becomes the basis for learning, rather than a source of blame and humiliation.

Increasingly, and within all sectors of the economy, coaching – sometimes called cognitive coaching – is becoming more and more widely adopted to solve this exact issue. A coach in this context is someone who develops energy and commitment in the people they work with to identify and act, for themselves, in a way that makes their situation better – be it work or personal.

A coach stays in the blue brain and lifts their coachee up into the same state through listening fully without judgement. Coachees can then face up to challenging or difficult situations with all their faculties available to them. The coach then asks questions that help the coachee to clarify how they should act to improve their situation. In the red brain we cannot find creative, collaborative solutions, and we don't believe they would work anyway. Being held in the blue brain, accompanied with gentle probing, allows us to determine what to do next and have the confidence to do it.

Coaches are gradually building self-determination in the people they work with. Coachees become used to deciding for themselves what to do, acting and seeing both successes and failures. Successes are celebrated and failures are learned from.

The very act of coaching is also developmental for the coach; after all, they are spending many hours per week holding themselves in the blue brain, strengthening their ability to stay there. They are also connecting deeply with other people, meeting their own need for connection.

Learning to coach or being coached are both ways to build our capacity to support the self-determination of our children. When it is modelled to us, we can more easily model it to our children. There are many books on coaching and in most workplaces coaching of this type is increasingly accessible. This is good for us and good for our children.

The importance of parents

University of Michigan psychology professor Barbara Smuts recounted the following story in *Sex and friendship in baboons*: "While studying wild baboons in Kenya, I once stumbled upon an infant baboon huddled in the corner of a cage at the local research station. A colleague had rescued him after his mother was strangled by a poacher's snare. Although he was kept in a warm, dry spot and fed milk from an eyedropper, within a few hours his eyes had glazed over: he was cold to the touch and seemed barely alive. We concluded he was beyond help. Reluctant to let him die alone, I took his tiny body to bed with me. A few hours later I was awakened by a bright-eyed infant bouncing on my stomach. My colleague pronounced a miracle."

Much has been written about the importance of a baby's first few years as a foundation for a successful and happy life. Even in the womb, a baby takes its cues from its mother as to what the outside world is like. A baby becomes used to its mother's sounds, as hearing develops in the womb well before childbirth, and recognises its mother from a range of other noises and other human voices. A baby needs its mother.

Operating in the blue brain as an expectant mother is the ideal setting for a baby to grow. Of course, this is easier said than done: it's difficult not to become anxious if something seems amiss with the pregnancy – just as it's difficult to always eat the right food, for example. We are where we are, and we do the best we can.

Once born, the baby needs to build a strong bond with a parent who provides love and affection. The baby will automatically respond to the parent, but it is up to the parent to initiate the relationship in a way that is healthy for the baby. A baby needs love that is not conditional. They need a mother or father who pays full attention to their child, free of judgement or comparison and, whatever the baby does, responds with kindness and compassion. As we will see in chapter 8, behaving in this way is not only ideal for the child but is also the means by which we can cause our own red brain to fade away. It is hard to behave this way with adults, and with growing children; but babies are built to attract this type of attention – it's why they are incredibly cute!

The ideal conditions for a baby to grow healthily are for both parents to act fully as adults with each other, with other siblings and especially with the new baby. Falling in love and starting a family is nature's way of showing us what the ideal conditions for a child really are: parents unconditionally accepting each other, responding always with kindness and compassion. Parents behaving in this way with their baby is the ideal environment for healthy growth.

In one sense, it is as simple as that; yet we know it is not that simple. We have all been brought up with an active red brain and a baby who does not do as we want can trigger it just as much as any other irritant. A baby might cry, have colic, or reject the milk being offered; this is just the way babies are. Red brain triggering in the mother (or another carer) has nothing to do with the baby, per se, and everything to do with the adult. Accepting the baby as they are will help prevent our red brain from triggering.

We owe it to our children to give them the best possible start in life. We can have the biggest impact when they are completely dependent on us; how we behave can, literally, shape their whole lives.

Biologically, babies are designed to pay attention to adults, so they will prefer those who behave like adults rather than people who are not authentic. Except for a parent. A baby instinctively recognises that its mother or father is key to its long-term survival and they will go out of their way not to disappoint or let this person down. Because of this, it can be easy to behave poorly with a young child – being irritable or suddenly blowing up; the child will not abandon us, where an older child or an adult might.

If a parent is only affectionate towards their child when the child behaves in a way they like, it's difficult for the child to feel truly accepted for who they are and to become self-determining. Instead, the child is more likely to be susceptible to outside influences and an active red brain as they grow into adulthood.

The bottom line is we can best avoid creating a red brain in our children by operating in the blue brain as much as possible ourselves. Some points that might help:

- Accept that being a parent is not easy: your children will challenge you, but that is OK.

- Remember that children want to be self-determining: they want to do things their way, not your way (it's not personal, as they say).

- Children don't reason the way adults do, and that's OK; accepting that they see the world in a different way can make it easier to accommodate their behaviour.

- Don't beat yourself up if your red brain triggers: it happens. The trick is to work to reduce future triggering.

- Have strategies for what do when the red brain does trigger (see chapters 2 and 5).

- Strengthening your blue brain (see chapter 6) will help you to stay there more of the time.

- Establishing regular habits of meditation and mindfulness will help to systematically reduce the effect of your own red brain.

We can still make amends

So, what happens if we didn't know all this when our first babies were born? Can we make amends, so to speak? My son, Duncan, was eight years old when he tried to cut his throat with a plastic knife. He grazed his skin – no actual harm done – but it was a wake-up call. He had been having behavioural problems at school and had fallen behind in school work; he was at the bottom of his reading group. Many years later he told me it was like standing on the edge of a cliff and it was just easier to fall off than it was to step back. It's scary that an eight-year-old would have such thoughts.

During the time that he was growing up I worked in senior corporate roles and travelled regularly around Australia and in Asia. I frequently left home early, came back late, and often spent one or more nights away. Duncan was our third child, with a four-year gap between him and his two sisters, who were closer in age. For whatever reason, the girls had grown up very easily. I suspect the novelty of having children had not yet worn off, so we paid more attention to the girls. I think we assumed that Duncan would follow in their footsteps without us having to do too much. I don't think I can avoid admitting to poor parenting on my part.

So, I had a wake-up call, just when I was working in my spare time with a local school to try and understand what made outstanding teachers so effective. I understood that it had something to do with listening, but I did not really know what. I had no other strategies, so I decided to try my best at listening. Whenever Duncan wanted to speak to me, I would get down to the same level and pay as much attention as I could to what he was trying to say. Similarly, if I needed to speak to him I would get to his level and pay attention to his responses.

After a few weeks, there was a noticeable change in his behaviour. I continued to apply what I was learning about listening (and applied it to my daughters, and wife too) and he continued to progress. To cut a long story short, by the end of primary school he won the school prize for English, and he could reflect on his own behaviour then modify it (in a way I have rarely seen in adults, let alone in a twelve-year-old).

Whenever I think of this story I reflect on how lucky I was; and how easy it would have been to try to shape his behaviour using reward and punishment – with, I am sure, disastrous outcomes for him – rather than to listen.

Research shows that a damaged child (or poorly parented, as in this case) only needs one adult to genuinely care for them to bring them back to a normal development trajectory. It is not too late to help our children become more self-determining and to reach adulthood with no red brain or a very much enfeebled one. Recognise that controlled motivation – reward and punishment – is the thing to avoid: it kills self-determination. Just as we can reduce the impact of our red brains, and (as we will learn in the next chapter) cause them to fade away completely, wherever a child is at in their development we can help them do the same.

Chapter 8
How to get out of the red brain III – eliminating it altogether

IS IT POSSIBLE TO MAKE the red brain go away altogether? I believe it is. In 2006 I developed a cognitive coaching methodology with my colleague Andrew Mowat, based on my observations of outstanding teachers. Like any inexperienced coach, I struggled with keeping my mind quiet as I listened to my coachee: random thoughts would surface; sudden comparisons would bring up floods of memories; I'd feel an urge to provide advice, just have a conversation, or make a sly attempt to judge. Gradually, through practice and using focused-attention meditation, I found that I could keep my mind quiet for a whole session and I began to feel shifts taking place within me, as though I had taken a step up in my acceptance and appreciation of the other person. I remember thinking this was good for me.

I also noticed that I was less anxious about things; in fact, I used to joke that I'd become anxious about why wasn't I anxious – a sort of second-order anxiety. It was about this time, early 2011, that I began to think that maybe I could go the next step and remove anxiety altogether. I began applying the skills I was using as a coach – listening with a quiet mind – to other parts of my work life and discovered that my mind could stay quiet for most of the time. I realised that I was practising mindfulness and investigated a bit further, so I could apply it more systematically. I began seeking out red brain triggers so that I could extinguish them.

I also realised that I had to apply the same practices to my personal life – much harder to do, as many habits and responses were laid down decades ago. This was the hardest part, in fact.

One morning in February 2017 I woke up with the feeling that something had changed. It gradually dawned on me that my red brain had gone. My mind was quiet, there was no negative self-talk – in fact, I had no memories of ever having had such talk – and I felt calm. I kept catching myself feeling joyful, and noticing that all my muscles were relaxed – as happens when we are in the right place, at the right time, doing the right thing.

Does this mean all triggers have gone? I think so. I surprise myself at times at how unconcerned I am when things don't go to plan or even disastrously wrong. This doesn't mean I ignore such events; the opposite, in fact, as I now respond fully present rather than being distracted by anxieties about the future or worries about the past. So, it can be done.

Having a red brain constrains and limits us, so making the effort to cause it to fade away completely is worth it. But how long does it take for a red brain to fade away, if we set out seriously to achieve that? Consider a child: at ten years old, the childhood mind is in full control and the adult mind is about to emerge as a separate mind state. In many pre-industrial, non-hierarchical societies, children would go through rites of passage at the age of fifteen or sixteen when they were considered to be adult or on the threshold of full adulthood. If we assume that the childhood mind had faded away by this point, then we are talking about five or six years for this fading away to take place.

As adults with a red brain, largely under control but still present, how likely is it that removing the red brain altogether will take more or less time? It is hard to say. For the fading away to occur in an adult, very substantial changes need to happen throughout the body; not just a change at the top but a root-and-branch change at the cellular level. For example, when we are anxious our muscles contract; free of anxiety, our muscles relax. Cells have memory of what they have done in the past, so the tensions built up through multiple contractions need to be released, and this takes time.

I personally began moving down this track seriously in February 2011 and my red brain had finally faded by February 2017, six years later. I did not know what I was doing when I began, but stumbled upon the necessary practices. It was only some years after starting that I realised the power of what I was doing and why, and could become more systematic about it.

An adult who believes they can cause their red brain to fade, and who puts in the required effort, may be able to achieve this change in less than six years, but it's hard to say for certain.

Preliminary practices: meditation and mindfulness

We saw in chapter 5 that we can begin to manage and modulate red brain triggering using meditation and mindfulness practices. Focused meditation helps us to limit random memories appearing unprompted in our minds, which generate negative feelings such as anxiety or guilt.

Through mindfulness, we learn to change the way we respond when something triggers our red brain. Rather than falling into the full red brain response, we are able to stop it from cascading and return to a calmer state. We feel good about ourselves when we choose a response that is better for us and for others, rather than succumbing to behaviour we might feel bad about. Mindfulness helps us to respond in adaptive, rather than maladaptive, ways in a range of circumstances.

Furthermore, practising mindfulness in the presence of red brain triggers enables our brain to modify the memories at the root of the trigger, and replace them with neutral or positive feelings. Over time we can reduce the number of things that are able to trigger our red brain.

Meditation and mindfulness are useful practices; mindfulness, in particular, is a very powerful tool in helping to bring the red brain under our control. Yet, we still have a red brain.

The practice of encounter

It is encounter that allows the red brain to finally fade away. Where meditation and mindfulness are solitary, encounter is a social practice: we do it in the presence of, and engaged with, someone else.

We practise encounter when we pay full attention to another without judgement or comparison, responding with kindness and compassion whatever the other person says or does. Paying full attention means that our conscious mind is quiet; we allow everything we see and hear to flow, unfiltered, into our brains.

This activates the right hemisphere and its way of paying attention to the world, since the right hemisphere connects to things beyond the self. Our attention on the other person stimulates their right hemisphere, which, in turn, further encourages our own. This mutual activation of each other's right hemispheres means that we achieve a state of genuine empathy and trust, and new information can flow uninhibited into our neural networks.

We are social creatures; we have evolved to grow healthily in the presence of, and deeply engaged with, other people. In a modern society, we have many opportunities to engage with other people throughout our day, which means we can build deep wells of trust and empathy by practising encounter at work or in a school, for example. Engaging with people who are different from us increases the new information flowing into our neural networks, which deepens our knowledge of the world as our brain finds patterns in, and connections with, the new information.

It is not possible to practise encounter when we dislike someone, or feel intimidated, or superior, or inferior. All these emotions arise from our red brain being triggered. This is why meditation and mindfulness are necessary preliminary practices: they allow us to be in the presence of another without our red brain triggering; then, if it begins to, we can choose to let it subside.

When we fully engage using encounter, no triggering is possible. Put another way, if we respond always with kindness and compassion – with concern for the other uppermost in our minds – there is no space for our red brain to throw up anxieties or concerns.

The practice of encounter creates the ideal environment for another's growth. This means that, if we practise encounter with children, they will be less likely to develop a red brain. Moreover, it will create the conditions for our own red brain to fade away. Thus, the practice of encounter is valuable to both giver and receiver of the practice.

Teachers who practise encounter

In chapter 6 I described outstanding teachers I had come across. I believe that what makes them so successful is the practice of encounter. An outstanding teacher has no discipline problems, delivers above-average outcomes and causes children to engage with the work that they set. On average, successful adults can remember two such teachers from their own schooling (which makes such teachers about one in twenty of all teachers).

When engaging with an individual student, an outstanding teacher is fully focused on the wellbeing of the student and listens to them using sustained attention. This means that, whatever the child says or does, there is no change in the teacher's positive regard for the child. In particular, they do not judge the student or compare them with other children.

The student so values this experience, albeit unconsciously, that they want it to continue and will go out of their way not to disappoint or let down the teacher. In short, the student becomes focused on the wellbeing of the teacher. If the teacher is technically competent, which is usually the case with such teachers, then they will propose the right work for the student to engage in and the student will willingly do it to the best of their ability. Even if the student does not find the work interesting or enjoyable, they are motivated to do it well because they value the connection with their teacher (note the absence of reward or punishment; the student is self-motivated to do the work). This leads to the best learning outcomes.

Optimal growth and optimal outcomes: this is why such teachers have a big effect on us. Encounter is not just good for the students, the practice of encounter in the classroom is the ideal environment for the teacher to thrive. The teacher is surrounded by twenty or so young people who are offering unconditional acceptance of the teacher; who listen, who respond thoughtfully, who visibly thrive in the teacher's presence. This environment reinforces the blue brain mind state and any residual red brain can fade away.

There's an important distinction between a very competent teacher who has good relationships with their students, and a teacher who practises encounter. Students of the first teacher will be compliant most of the time and, although their teacher usually responds with kindness, the students know at the back of their minds that if they step outside a certain boundary the teacher's response will *not* be kind. Neither party receives the benefits from encounter.

Encounter in all aspects of life

For the red brain to fade away completely, we need to practise encounter in every aspect of life. It is often easier to practise in professional life: when we change jobs or roles we can decide to behave differently with our new colleagues than with our former colleagues. This is particularly true in a school, as each year a new cohort of students arrives, and a teacher can choose to behave differently with little risk of embarrassment.

It can be much harder to practise encounter in our personal lives, particularly if we have been with a partner for a substantial period. Many of our responses will have become hardwired through being repeated over and over. It is much harder to change our behaviour with someone who knows us well, and it is much harder to change deep-seated habits. In my own case, I think I took longer than I needed to, as I focused mainly on my professional life, only applying the learnings to my personal life when I realised that this was not enough.

The one-on-one engagement of encounter can be codified into cognitive coaching – as either a formal or informal process; coaching is becoming increasingly popular in all walks of life, including in schools, as mentioned in the previous chapter. The characteristics of coaching emulate what an outstanding teacher does with a student; in coaching, a leader systematically uses encounter with a colleague to help their own red brain to fade away and to help the other along the same path.

Modern organisations are based around teams, groupings of people who work together to achieve something they could not achieve on their own. High-performing teams are characterised by high levels of psychological safety, created through the leader modelling kindness and compassion with each team member; everyone knows that they can speak up without fear of embarrassment or humiliation. Opportunities for encounter are emerging more and more, and showing themselves to be the pathway to higher performance.

It may feel that we are being very productive if our mind is racing as we are in conversation with someone else, and that having a quiet mind, placing all our attention on the other person, makes us less effective. We think, if my mind is not active now then I will miss what is happening. But there lies the fallacy. Having our conscious mind quiet does not mean that our mind is quiet; far from it: we hear more, we are more aware and our unconscious mind makes more connections.

Through encounter we become more connected

When we practise encounter, we – being somewhat competent, somewhat self-determining – connect with someone else who is also somewhat competent and somewhat self-determining. Encounter enables us to connect more fully with more people.

Paying full attention to another person – using sustained, rather than focused, attention – causes them to feel valued; they feel more positive and optimistic. Their desire to honour this attention means that they respond thoughtfully: they do not want to say something stupid or irrelevant to someone who is paying such attention to them. Their thinking opens up and they have more time for consideration – more time for choice – before responding.

As they realise that whatever they say will not be judged or compared – they will not be embarrassed or humiliated – then responses can become ever more authentic and fully self-determined. The person says what they really think, unconstrained by anxieties or fears.

The first person then chooses to further increase the happiness of the other or to decrease their suffering. That is, their response is wholly focused on the needs of the other, rather than their own. They don't try to better the other person's story or boost their own self-esteem by recounting something that puts them in a good light. In encounter, we practise not allowing any of our own anxieties or personal failings to determine our responses.

We are clearly connecting with another person when we practise encounter. Because we use sustained attention, new information flows into our neural networks; we are, literally, more connected as a consequence of this encounter. As we find patterns and make connections, sudden insights can lead to deeper self-awareness, or ideas that can only arise by combining what we know with what we are learning from the other.

The benefits of encounter flow both ways. The person receiving the attention feels valued and listened to (both of which activate their blue brain), leading them to become more thoughtful and optimistic. The one giving, so to speak, gains greater understanding of their own self and has creative or new ideas; and their red brain becomes that little bit less able to take hold.

Our need to belong

Through encounter we become more connected to self and more connected to another. We know ourselves better when we connect deeply with another. But connection also encompasses two other elements: connection to place – being grounded; and connection to something larger than ourselves – connection to purpose.

At the most fundamental level, when everything is up in the air, we need to belong. For children severely damaged by a poor upbringing, the very first thing they crave is a safe place: a place where they are physically safe; somewhere they can return to and be safe. In the times of our hunter-gatherer ancestors, being excluded from the family group usually meant death. To survive and thrive we needed to belong.

Although we live today in societies where we can, seemingly, belong anywhere, the underlying drive to belong is still there. When it is met, another part of what we need to grow healthily falls into place: joy is our response to being in the right place, at the right time, doing the right thing. In other words, we experience joy when we find where we belong; and we belong where we are unconditionally accepted. Accepted for who we are and as we are.

The final element of connection is connection to purpose: what should I be doing that gives my life meaning? The first answers to this are usually focusing less on external drivers of behaviour, or extrinsic goals, and focusing more on internal drivers or intrinsic goals. We can live well without another car, but I will live much less well if I am estranged from my daughter.

The more we practise encounter the more our brains re-wire themselves to remove imposed behaviours and other unhelpful habits and the healthier we become in terms of being able to approach life with equanimity and calm, and with joy in our hearts. We take pleasure in simple things that we freely choose to do.

To live well we need to do something of value – something that we value – that allows us to demonstrate and grow our competence. This may be the work we are doing now, or we may gradually find something that suits us better. Whatever it is, if we value it and we do it well, it will be a source of great satisfaction.

Our purpose gradually emerges, so that we are driven to become our best selves and that all we do gradually becomes in service to that. Our best selves develop in the service of others so that we are grounded in family and community.

We benefit from encounter

The reason we practise encounter is because it is good for us. It is clearly of benefit to the other as well; and, even when they do not respond with encounter, the benefits are great enough to us to continue the practice. When both parties practise encounter then the conversation can deepen; we relax, and we are suffused with this feeling that we call joy.

Falling in love is the commonest manifestation of this experience. Everything that our loved one does is fascinating; we pay full attention to them, without judgement or comparison, and we respond always with kindness and compassion. We practise encounter.

M Scott Peck asserted in his best-selling 1978 book, *The road less travelled,* that falling in love is an evolutionary trick to induce a couple to produce a child and raise it to adulthood; something they would not do of their own accord. In other words, he implies that falling in love is an aberrant state and, within a matter of months, we drop back into our normal, everyday state of mind where we begin to judge and compare our spouse, and find them wanting.

My view is the reverse. Falling in love is not a trick to make us do something we might not otherwise do; rather, it is our body's way of showing us the ideal environment in which to bring up children. This is the blue brain in its finest expression. If we could keep it up, we would stay in that amazing state for the rest of our lives. Many people have experienced this feeling of being valued completely by another – being unconditionally loved – and reciprocating. In this state – a blue brain state – it is no effort to pay such attention, nor to refrain from judgement, nor to respond with kindness. It seems the most natural thing to do. Because it is.

What falling in love provides for us is a state of mind to aim for. We know it is possible because we have experienced it before. We now need to put in the work through meditation, mindfulness and encounter to rewire our plastic brains and recreate this as a permanent state, rather than a temporary state to ensure continuation of the species. Meditation helps us to become more competent through being in flow, while mindfulness allows us to be more self-determining (choosing our responses to external triggers). Both these practices help our brains rewire themselves to meet these innate drives more closely. Encounter enables us to meet our need for connection: through encounter, we connect more deeply with others and ourselves, with place, and with our purpose – what truly drives us.

Some history behind the practice of encounter

Meditation and mindfulness come out of the Buddhist tradition (and are based on earlier Hindu traditions). Buddhism also incorporates a set of practices called loving kindness or compassion, or sometimes in the scientific literature, ethical enhancement. These practices are also solitary: we imagine being kind to other people – and there is some benefit to this – but these ancient traditions do not go the next step and move into social practices. The societies from which they arose were highly stratified and it was simply impossible for people at different status levels to practise loving-kindness face to face. Brahmins (the Indian priest class) were simply prohibited from having anything to do with "untouchables" (the lowest, pariah class). Similarly, it is unimaginable that a Chinese mandarin would practise loving-kindness face to face with any of the millions of peasants pressed into corvée labour. Imagine anyone of the Samurai class in Japan doing the same with a peasant!

So these traditions focused on developing as individuals to manage and modulate their red brains – but they still had red brains. They did not incorporate the last and most powerful step of developing the self together with others who are different from us, and causing the red brain to fade away.

It took the Christians to stumble across the practice of encounter, through the teachings of Christ and the very particular social and demographic conditions that allowed it to spread within a slave-based empire. With the Christian perspective came the idea of perfectibility: that we could become less angry, less jealous, less selfish over time. The notion that master and slave could both participate equally in a Christian assembly – and that interactions were based on offering loving kindness to each other – was revolutionary.

Being revolutionary, in and of itself, is no guarantee of success. Very specific social and demographic conditions allowed these ideas to spread. One salient condition was the position of women. It's estimated that, at the time that Christianity began its spread, there were one hundred and thirty men for every hundred women in the Roman Empire. This was due, in part, to the practice of female infanticide. A second cause was the death of women through abortion: a girl or woman who fell pregnant in circumstances that were inappropriate – from the male perspective – would simply be ordered to have an abortion by the ranking male member of the household; sterility and death were common outcomes.

Girls were married young – often before reaching puberty – to men much older than themselves. Many young men were reluctant to marry as, with a paucity of girls, they were uncomfortable being with females in normal social settings and being tied to one was not seen as being attractive. The frequenting of prostitutes was socially acceptable; it was also common and accepted for men to have sex with boys.

Sociologist Rodney Stark set out to understand how religions grow at the rate that Christianity did during its rise. Studying the Mormon religion, which has grown by forty per cent each decade over the past century, he concluded that conversion occurs because of attachment: we convert – mostly from religions or beliefs that have lost their force – because our friends or family have converted. Women tend to convert first – due to their greater attachment, while committed believers or committed non-believers tend not to convert.

In the early Christian groups that began forming in the Roman Empire, the tendency for women to convert first meant that they had greater presence, and therefore status, in these groups than in Roman society more generally. Christians were also opposed to infanticide and artificial forms of birth control, which led to them having more gender-balanced, and larger, families. With an excess of marriageable women within the Christian sects, women were encouraged to marry pagans – the one proviso being that children be brought up as Christians. There was no concern that Christian women would reconvert; it was assumed that pagan husbands would eventually convert instead.

Two major epidemics ravaged the Roman Empire during the rise of Christianity (thought to be smallpox and measles). Each lasted about fifteen years and led to forty per cent mortality amongst pagans and ten per cent mortality amongst Christians. Why this difference? The Christians nursed and cared for each other, whereas the pagans did not. All things being equal, two sick people will have very different survival outcomes if one is looked after, provided with food and water and cared for, and the other is not. Christians cared for people in their own attachment networks, which would have included pagans as well. Once the epidemics were over the Christians would have had more intact networks of connections, whereas surviving pagans would have fewer.

The relationship between pagans and their gods was quite different than between Christians and their god. Pagan gods had no interest in humankind but could be persuaded to help an individual, family or community through offerings and sacrifices. There was no urging by such gods that believers should care for each other, and in a stratified society looking after yourself and those close to you was as far as things went.

Christians, on the other hand, saw everyone as children of God, each deserving kindness and compassion. Thus, they would go out of their way to help those they met. People saw that their friends or family were living in a way that was somehow better and so they would, over time, convert as well. Women, particularly, saw that this new way of living was better for them.

Clearly, within a few generations, Christianity had moved away from its early beginnings and, two thousand years later, little remains in the mainstream of the revolutionary concept of unconditional love. It is encouraging to note that the current Pope, Francis, is promoting the idea of encounter as the core to the Christian life within the Roman Catholic Church.

What the early Christians practised was encounter, the most powerful of the three practices we have discussed. Like meditation and mindfulness, encounter is a simple practice: whenever we are in the presence of another human we pay full attention to them, free of judgement or comparison; whatever they say or do, we respond with kindness – a desire to increase their happiness – or compassion – a desire to reduce their suffering. Over time, this practice causes the red brain to fade away and we become fully healthy.

Living without a red brain

The early Christians experienced how much better life could be with less red brain and more blue brain and the satisfaction – joy – that comes from being truly connected to others through the practice of encounter. Their members designated as saints were those who operated always – or almost always – in the blue brain. Initially, saints were living exemplars of what was possible and what others could aim for. Remember, too, that all this was occurring within a slave-based empire that encouraged the persistence of red brain behaviours.

When the red brain is gone, we are free of negative internal narratives and our minds are quiet places with a single, helpful voice. This means that our minds are no longer full of intruding thoughts and emotions; we no longer play events over in our minds, making our own roles more heroic – not saying the pejorative comment (that we did in fact say), responding with a humorous riposte (where, in reality, we were left feeling intimidated and blustering).

However, this does not mean that there is nothing going on in our minds. Without the red brain our unconscious mind can work unhindered – taking in continuous streams of information through our senses from the people, events and environments around us and making meaning from them. This meaning emerges non-verbally – through our intuition: we know what we ought to do because it feels like the right thing to do; critically, this feeling emerges from a considered view of what is best for our organism and for those people and places we are connected with. We call on our internal voice to articulate these intuitions so that we can make sense of them ourselves and communicate and share them with others.

We are free of hesitation; our minds are less cluttered; and we respond more intuitively from a space inside us that is deeply ethically grounded. These are the immediate benefits of not having a red brain.

In a "blue brain world" people unhesitatingly do what they believe to be right, act with courage, and affirm what is best within them, feeling great satisfaction in doing so. Beliefs about what is right emerge from a deeply felt sense of being connected and grounded and having the collective interest at heart. Being calm and unassuming is the norm.

When I was at university in the UK I became involved in the Officers Training Corps, which provided an introduction to military training and an opportunity to experience military life through weekend exercises and an annual camp.

During training exercises I noticed that one of my fellow officer cadets, Dave, always seemed to do the right thing without hesitation. A situation might arise where someone needed to speak up or act and as I, and others, were hesitating, deciding if we should do it (What would people think? What if it is the wrong thing to do or say?), Dave, without a moment's hesitation, would just say or do it, in an unassuming way. If he was wrong, he would also immediately admit to his mistake without embarrassment or hesitation. Even at eighteen I recognised this behaviour as being unusual but, equally, to be admired.

We both joined the army and went through officer training together; subsequently, we joined different regiments. A year or so later a fellow officer in my regiment, Barry, asked me if I had known Dave at Cambridge. He asked what he was like and I shared Dave's uncanny ability to always do what was right. He told me that he and Dave had gone through the three-day selection process for officer training together. The process involved a series of group activities ranging from group discussions on particular topics to outdoor problem-solving exercises that the group completed together. While participants were not told how they were being assessed, they were observed for leadership qualities.

Barry told me that whenever Dave's group was involved in an activity, all the instructors came out to watch. Curious, at the end of the three days Barry asked one of the instructors why; the instructor replied that they rate successful candidates as A, B, or C and that almost all successful candidates are rated C. They thought that Dave was going to be an A, so everyone was excited to see. Apparently, Dave was rated a B. Which makes me wonder what an A would be like.

Chapter 9
What this means for our schools

SCHOOLS HAVE A POWERFUL EFFECT on the shape of society. The introduction of state compulsory schooling in the early nineteenth century – first by the Prussians and subsequently adopted around the world – was the first systematic attempt by state rulers to break the connection between children and their families and communities. Any sense of self-determination was replaced with obedience to authority.

In the first iteration of state compulsory education, schools used harsh discipline and rote learning to build the competencies needed for industrialising societies – reading, writing and arithmetic – and the capacity to complete repetitive tasks without complaint. These methods effectively suppressed or severely stunted the emergence of the adult mind so that most of the population were obedient and dependent on authority figures. Such adults did not have a red brain so much as they continued with the childhood mind in its entirety, with both its positive and shadow sides.

However, such a society still needed doctors, administrators and engineers; a small minority were developed so that their adult mind (blue brain) emerged alongside the red brain, which their upbringing encouraged to persist into adulthood. These adults could fulfil the demanding roles required of them, but could not challenge the status quo. Superior schools and then universities were reserved to develop selected young people in this way.

This basic framework held in place up until the First World War and then changed substantially after the Second World War, shifting emphasis so that the small minority became most of the population: schools today tend to produce adults with two brains and a body of acquired knowledge. This model was hugely successful in raising post-war living standards. Meanwhile, the welfare state provided basic needs for those temporarily unemployed or sick, or no longer able to work.

Through the nineteenth century the state largely needed the physical abilities of most of its population. This changed in the second half of the twentieth century, when the ability to apply an acquired body of knowledge became increasingly important.

In the twenty-first century, we need to be able to solve complex problems; we need to use existing knowledge and expand on it, then apply both to new situations. This is not achievable without increasing degrees of self-determination and deeper connections with self and others.

After two hundred years of trying to limit and control human expression, our societies now need people who are fully developed; who can think, create and collaborate – and continue to grow through adulthood. We need a population of adults who operate in the blue brain, unhindered by a red brain.

Schools are how society replicates itself. As societies evolve in response to technological, demographic, political or other changes, schools change too – but with a lag. It is only when the shape of the changes becomes clear that schools can change to accommodate them.

We see efforts being made everywhere in the world to improve education so it can produce young adults with twenty-first-century skills – essentially, young adults who operate in the blue brain. This implies that societies everywhere have changed further than we think, and schools are now striving to catch up. Today we want our schools to create adults with the full capacity of adults.

The blue brain transforms education

In the presence of an outstanding teacher, a child grows in healthy ways towards this objective. Up until the age of about ten the childhood mind is in control; this mind state is self-centred and impulsive, is curious and emotional, and responds to rewards and punishments. It is this latter characteristic that a teacher operating in the blue brain can avoid using and abusing altogether.

Reward and punishment have long been associated with education to the extent that it seems a natural pairing. However, these extrinsic forms of motivation stifle autonomous motivation, which is the key to developing a blue brain. This means that we must eliminate the concept of rewards and punishments from education, and instead promote self-determination.

This is possibly the most fundamental shift. When researchers began looking at human behaviour and motivation in the early part of the twentieth century, most took the view that *all* human behaviour was shaped by external stimuli. If you wanted a given behaviour, you just needed to design the correct reward or punishment.

This was not an unreasonable view, as the population they were observing had been trained to lack self-determination; instead, to be obedient. It was only in the 1950s that an alternative view emerged with research being conducted on university students – a group who, by this time, were developing self-determination to a certain degree in response to the social and economic needs of the time.

If we accept that rewards and punishments must be eliminated from education, the implication is that our education systems need to support teaching staff to make the shift towards operating more and more as full adults themselves. Teachers who operate always in the blue brain, and are autonomously motivated to pursue their own growth, will inspire their students to do the same.

There are two ways to achieve this over time. One is to recruit and develop pre-service teachers who operate in the blue brain from day one of their teaching careers. This is a longer-term strategy, as it will take time to build up a critical mass of teachers who behave this way; indeed, changing the culture within teacher development programs may take as long as changing the culture in schools.

The other way is to recognise the importance of creating a blue brain culture at the school level and then focus on changing behaviours, attitudes, policies, processes and organisational structures to achieve this. A lot needs to change.

Clearly, these two approaches are mutually reinforcing. All but the most resilient new teachers will conform to the existing school culture so, for the development of pre-service teachers to be successful, school cultures need to change as well. Of course, they are changing, but slowly and intermittently.

Teaching as a profession

What these deep-seated changes mean is that teaching is becoming a profession. The change occurring now is more profound than the change that followed the world wars; that was a change in content and activity, but was not about who teachers were, as people.

There is a simple rule of thumb for defining a profession and thus distinguishing between a profession and a non-profession. This rule is that the work produced by the professional is not the primary basis for their evaluation, whereas the product or service produced by the non-professional *is* the basis for their evaluation. For example, a production manager is evaluated on the quantity and quality of physical products; a bricklayer is judged on the quality of a brick wall, and the time spent building it.

The primary means of assessing a professional is the person's attitudes, behaviours and skills – their professional practice. A lawyer can continue to be highly regarded even though they lose their client's case. Their client would still use them again for their next case because they have been impressed by their skills as a lawyer, despite losing the case. A patient dies, yet the doctor is seen as a hero. Professionals inspire confidence in their clients and it is this that causes the client to continue as a client even though a measured outcome may be much less than desired.

Some early research I did with schools was to organise a poll of parents across a range of schools to ask them to describe their ideal school and ideal teacher. From the results, seventeen characteristics were identified that described the "ideal school". Teachers from seven schools then took individual parents through a process of ordering these characteristics according to which had most impact on their satisfaction with a school ("If you were choosing between two schools which things would most influence your choice?").

The order was very similar in each school, with six of the top seven relating to the attitudes or behaviours of teachers. They were: teachers encourage individual, all-round development of students; teachers are highly professional and capable; the school is a safe place for students, staff and parents; teachers listen and communicate effectively with students and parents; teachers are inspiring and enthusiastic; teachers have a genuine love for educating children; and teachers provide good role models and the school is strongly values based.

Although I did not understand this at the time, outstanding teachers would score highly on each of these characteristics, as would teachers in general who are operating in the blue brain. "Discipline" was ranked between nine and eleven, which makes sense: if teachers are inspiring and enthusiastic there will be few discipline problems. "Uniform" always came last – and by a long way.

Of the seventeen characteristics, none related to how well a parent's child was doing at school in terms of any measured learning outcome. This seemed odd at first so, with a subset of four schools, we took the satisfaction levels (that parents also provided along with the prioritisation exercise) and each school assessed the corresponding student in terms of how well they were doing at school on a scale from A to E. Interestingly, the principals of the four schools expected a high correlation between parent satisfaction levels and how well their children were doing at school.

Instead, we found only a very small correlation between parental satisfaction with a school and how well their child was doing. Thus, a parent with an A-grade student was almost as likely to be dissatisfied with the school as a parent with an E-grade student and vice versa.

This makes sense when we see that what drives parental satisfaction (after safety) are the attitudes and behaviours of teachers. Who teachers are matters more to parents than what they do. Parental satisfaction is driven by what their children need – that is, a teacher whose attitude and behaviour allows them to thrive.

So, if a teacher inspires confidence in a parent, however the child turns out is fine as the child is getting what they need to thrive, and the outcome is the best that can be expected. Yet, if a teacher does not inspire confidence in a parent, even if their child is an A-grade student, the parent will think: with a better teacher my child would do even better.

Based on this research, teaching is a profession: parents evaluate teachers on their attitudes and behaviours, not on their measurable outcomes.

When did teaching become a profession and why? In nineteenth-century education systems, teachers used harsh discipline and rote learning to produce habitual and obedient adults; they were disciplinarians, judged on the behaviour of their students – their output. The teacher was clearly not a professional; rather, a state employee.

The system that has dominated post-war education produces young people with two brains – one where they are at their best and one where they are not. In this system, too, the teacher created a façade to shape student behaviour ("don't smile before Easter" was a common Australian saying) and the teacher cannot be classified as a true professional, either.

So, it is the emergence of the third form of education – needed to develop twenty-first-century skills – that allows (and encourages) the childhood mind to fade away and develop the adult mind as the only continuing mind state, that is driving this shift into teachers becoming professionals. The childhood mind fades away when the child is continually in the presence of adults who model being in the adult mind (no red brains in sight!). Teachers in this context are professionals: who they are matters as much, or more, than what they do.

The emergence of a new system reflects a shift in education from being educator-centred to learner-centred; a shift from schooling to true education and a two-hundred-year journey for teachers from the non-professional to the professional.

This raises some obvious issues. First, if teaching is a profession, do teachers know what attitudes and behaviours inspire confidence in parents? Do they systematically develop them? And do appraisal systems monitor them? We know that the answers to these questions are no.

Second, if who they are is just as important as what they do, then managing, modulating and eventually removing their red brains becomes an integral part of teachers' professional development.

And, third, if teaching is becoming a profession, perhaps schools should be organised like professions, rather than like the businesses they are modelled on today.

Organisational structure

Business organisational structures were developed to efficiently marshal relatively static resources to achieve a planned outcome. Historically, these resources were people doing standardised tasks and the machines they worked on or with. The majority of people simply did as they were told; a small number – managers – may have been open to learning and further development.

For most of the last two hundred years this organisational model has been applied to schools, quite rationally, in fact. The vast bulk of people in a school – the students – were supposed to complete the work they were set in order to acquire specific knowledge and skills. Teachers, once they had developed suitable strategies for managing and teaching a class, remained relatively static in their teaching practice, providing more or less the same each year. A business organisational structure suited this teaching environment.

However, schools are now becoming – and seen as becoming – learning environments; we now want students, as well as acquiring knowledge and skills, to develop as rounded human beings. We want students to be learners; indeed, to be life-long learners. Considerable effort has gone into developing new curricula and new pedagogies that reflect the importance of building learning skills and working collaboratively.

Ideally, teachers would model learning to students. This happens more naturally with an organisational structure that stimulates learning – such as that of a professional service firm.

A three-tier structure is the classic format for professional services. Disparagingly, these tiers are sometimes referred to as "finders", "minders" and "grinders"; insulting as they might be, these labels do give a sense of what each level is accountable for.

"Finders" are the senior leaders who position their organisation within the world: defining the value it offers to stakeholders; ensuring that the work is of the right standard, and that the right people are recruited, developed and retained. This tier is largely strategic in nature.

"Minders" are the middle leaders who manage and lead the day-to-day work that the organisation does. They increase its value through coaching and mentoring, organising teams and initiating improvements. Middle leaders are the powerhouse of a professional firm: there are usually quite a lot of them; they still do not cost very much; they are highly formed professionals; and they are able to raise the productivity of the "grinders" – those who are new to the profession and who need to put in the hours to develop their capabilities as fast as possible.

Developing staff capability in schools

In top professional firms, staff develop the capability of middle leaders in around four years from entry. Salaries typically double, reflecting the high value that middle leaders bring. A large part of the value in a professional is their personal attributes: a teacher would learn technical skills in the classroom – as they do now – but, more importantly, would learn to operate fully in the blue brain, no matter what was thrown their way.

Professional firms become more valuable the more valuable each member becomes, so they are set up to ensure people develop at an optimal rate. You can see why this might be important for the education system that is emerging: we now want students to develop their capabilities fully and optimally. People develop by engaging in meaningful and challenging work that gets progressively more demanding as their capabilities develop. We understand how this applies to student learning, but it should be the same for professionals: teachers need to grow optimally as well, and model this to their students.

Another feature of professional services is that as people reach the upper side of their current tier they start to do the work of the tier above; when they can be counted upon to do that work reliably then they get the role. Thus, no one goes into a role that they do not know how to do. This avoids a major flaw in the business organisation model, whereby someone can take 18 months to come up to speed in a new role, and if the wrong person is put into the role, this might not be apparent for months, if not years.

If we compare a school with, say, a hundred professionals to a professional service firm of the same size, today, both would have senior leadership groups of about six to ten people. However, in the school, generally only one of those would be a principal. In the professional service firm, all members of the senior group would have the same ultimate accountability as a principal and therefore the same capability (as they only get the job when they can be counted upon to do it reliably). Looked at another way, the professional service model develops many more people capable of being principals; the current school organisational model generally only produces one.

Having half a dozen or more senior leaders in a school with the same capabilities as a principal would have a dramatic impact on a school – not least on the stress levels of principals. Further, if there is underdevelopment at the top, this is likely to be the pattern throughout; this means that classroom teachers would not develop as far or as fast as they can, which we have already observed.

If each large school had half a dozen senior leaders who were as capable as the principal and who worked collaboratively together for the good of the school, what a difference that would make. Couple that with increasing the number of outstanding teachers sixfold as well, from around five to thirty per cent, then we would have schools that were well on the way to meeting society's needs for the future.

This all suggests that a business organisation model – the current model in schools – is hindering rather than helping the changes that we want to see. The organisational model needs to support teachers to grow optimally so that they, in turn, model this to students.

Middle leaders in schools

As noted, senior leadership teams in schools are now typically six to ten strong, which is a substantial increase over the situation twenty years ago, where such a group might only be the principal, a deputy principal and a business manager. The larger groups are also making significant efforts to concentrate on strategic issues rather than the day-to-day operation, which typically occupied leaders in the past. This is moving in the direction of a professional model.

A focus on strategy allows leadership teams to rise above the day-to-day and focus on longer-term, substantive changes. This is a necessary step for the transformation that is taking place to be taken forward successfully. These leaders are now modelling a different way of behaving, more blue brain; more optimistic.

The widening gap between senior leaders and teaching staff opens the space for a middle leadership group to step up and provide day-to-day leadership to staff. Senior leaders today are trying to shift day-to-day operation to middle leaders, and realising that middle leaders lack the capacity to immediately take on this role. In effect, teachers in the classroom are not learning the skills to be middle leaders.

If a teacher spends their first years in the classroom learning to operate fully in the blue brain, then, when asked to start doing the work of a middle leader, they will already have the personal qualities required, and need only to acquire the management or other skills required for the role. As it stands today, most teachers can spend many years in the classroom yet lack the motivation and personal qualities to lead others. However, as blue brain behaviour occurs more and more in the classroom, more teachers will emerge from the classroom with the personal qualities to become middle leaders, increasing the overall capacity of middle leaders to fulfil their role.

Middle leaders would also be responsible for making sure that teams of teaching staff are collaborative and high performing. Essentially, this means creating and sustaining blue brain environments when teachers come together. Many teams today operate at the lower level of simple co-operation: people are there because there is something in it for them (or they are obliged to be there), and focus on getting their own needs met rather than contributing to meeting the needs of others (for example, ruminating on something that you just said to the meeting rather than paying full attention to the next contributor).

The middle leadership group should also have a common understanding of both the current state of teacher practice across the school, and of what good practice looks like in the twenty-first century – that is, teaching that develops skills that students need, that preferences formative assessment over summative assessment (which should be used sparingly) in order to stimulate intrinsic motivation and encourage differentiated work.

Collectively reflecting on the gap between current practice and ideal practice, middle leaders could then initiate improvements to raise the average practise across the school. This is a major departure from historic practice where a teacher could go into their classroom, shut the door, and no-one other than the children would know what was going on. Middle leaders should be able to be counted upon to ensure that practice continues to develop across the school in every class and for every teacher.

The importance of culture

The work that humans do is changing from being mainly algorithmic work – work that can be split into sequential steps, to being heuristic – requiring creativity, complex problem solving, collaboration, iterative solutions. In algorithmic work, no matter how complex it might appear to be, it is possible to develop a plan that can be executed step by step. In heuristic work this is not possible: the level of complexity precludes knowing, a priori, the steps to take; they must be worked out as you proceed towards a solution. Putting a person on the moon took ten years and was incredibly complicated, but each step could be planned and executed – with failures and setbacks, to be sure – but progress moved forward within planned parameters. Resolving human-induced climate change cannot be achieved in the same way. Any solution (and we are not even sure there is one) will be arrived at by a pathway that cannot be foreseen. This is heuristic work.

In simple algorithmic work, conversation is redundant. Instructions are given and there may be some dialogue to clarify what those instructions mean but, otherwise, this kind of work does not need conversation. When our current (post-war) education system was established, children were expected to work by themselves, not conversing with other students, for just this reason. As we were trained to take instruction without question, we were also trained to judge and compare what we heard from others. In judging, we compare what somebody has said with what we ourselves have learned: Does this match or not? If it does not, then the other person is simply labelled as wrong. There is no co-creation of a new idea from two different views.

We also compare what we are hearing to our own experience and bring up memories or instances that are similar. If a colleague complains of how their manager just spoke to them, I might bring up my own example of when they spoke to me in a similar way. What this means is that next time I see this manager this memory is likely to spring to mind, colouring how we interact; this memory may even be enough to trigger the red brain.

A lot of what passed for conversation in our workplaces was of this type. It is not helpful; in fact, it is unhealthy. In simple work, conversation is redundant, so it is not structured to support the work. A consequence is that unhealthy conversations can happen instead.

Heuristic work is grounded in conversation: genuine exchanges of views and ideas to fuel creativity and collaboration. A transition is necessary to move away from unhelpful conversation towards the rich conversations needed for this work. In effect, we need to shift to conversations about the work and move away from conversations that do not contribute either to the work or to employees' mental health.

To make this shift, leaders must refrain from taking part in such conversations themselves and model the sorts of conversations that are more helpful. Leaders can use informal coaching to help colleagues make decisions themselves, rather than simply telling them what to do. This develops self-determination and, gradually, local decisions are made without reference to the leader, which thus frees up the leader's time for other work. This shift in culture exactly parallels a move towards having less red brain and more blue brain.

Chapter 10
What this means for us

THIS IS TRULY A HISTORIC MOMENT. Ever since humans settled into agricultural communities we have been subject to controlled motivation that has developed and sustained the red brain–blue brain split. Although this was not good for individual humans, it has led to the developed world we see about us. It is difficult to say if things could have been any different, or if the urge to meet our physical needs by exploiting others was just too great for the minority to pass over. Or maybe it happened by chance, or desperation. Whatever the case, our industrial societies are based around the same controlled motivation of the majority by the minority.

But things are now changing. Machines can now do a very major part of the algorithmic work that needs physical movement and low-level cognitive skills. However, they cannot do heuristic work – the complex creative work that requires problem solving, often through collaboration.

A possible outcome of this change is that people who are no longer needed to do simple work are simply discarded in some way; and, ultimately, a large die-off of population takes place through war, disease, famine and despair. This is a direction that I do not want to see the world take; however, this conclusion is logically possible if we continue with the status quo.

The better outcome is that, with our basic needs met by the widespread use of robots and artificial intelligence, humans can do work that is both of high value, and fulfilling. What will that work be? We don't really know – except that it will be complex in nature and require people to operate in the blue brain.

We have had thousands of years to become accustomed to living with two brains, yet the desire to live better has never left us. Prophets, philosophers and saints have all regularly appeared with practices and ideas that have fought against our situation, and through their own example have shown that things could be different. Every moment a child is born who does not know that this is the way things are organised, and naturally strives to grow fully, only held back by the adults and systems around them.

Organised religions such as Hinduism and Buddhism went some way towards managing and modulating the red brain, but in the service of their host societies, which were rigidly hierarchical in nature. With the emergence of Christianity encounter became widely practised, offering oppressed citizens within the slave-based, patriarchal Roman Empire a better way of living.

Once Christianity became the official religion of the Roman Empire, however, the practice of encounter faded away from the mainstream and Christianity became just another religion supporting the status quo. The powerful had adopted Christianity and being kind to others came to be seen as a sign of weakness; rituals continued but not the spirit.

In our more recent history, a consequence of state compulsory schooling has been the two-brain state being created and sustained in a much more systematic way. Because it has been sustained over two centuries, it appears that this state is just human nature; but, of course, it is not. Now, for the first time in settled human history, having the average young person operating fully in the blue brain is increasingly seen as desirable, indeed essential, for the future success of our society itself.

We must not let this opportunity pass.

So, what can we do?

In every part of our lives we can strive to move towards the blue brain. Become a blue brain parent, a blue brain spouse, a blue brain leader, a blue brain colleague, a blue brain friend. Form a blue brain movement.

At its heart, such a movement is based around the practice of encounter. This means making conscious effort to change the way we behave with everyone around us: when we engage with others, we need to pay full attention to them without judging or comparing and, whatever they say or do, respond with kindness and compassion.

This is not easy to do. We have been conditioned to judge and compare; our red brains trigger when someone does not meet our standards. We must recognise this for what it is: the negative feelings that arise (and that we interpret as dislike, or intimidation, or contempt for the other) are just memories of past events with these feelings attached.

Practising mindfulness and encounter will stimulate our brains to progressively extinguish the negative emotions associated with these memories and replace them with neutral or positive feelings. Eventually, we can engage with the person without negative feelings arising. This is the true power of mindfulness and encounter: it allows us to reprogram ourselves so that we are not at the mercy of our memories; we have choice over how we respond.

Wherever we can, we must separate ourselves from the grip of controlled motivation. The belief that it is normal and appropriate to induce or coerce others to do as we want needs to be rejected once and for all. Let's engage with people, state our case, propose our course of action and let people decide for themselves what they want to do. As individuals we must resist being controlled, refuse to play the part that controlled motivation assigns us, choose our own course.

We are at the beginning of a new age. Humanity is facing serious and complex threats; yet I am optimistic that these global problems, coupled with the striving that young people have to develop into healthy, self-determining adults, will force a change in the way we organise our societies.

Getting there will not be easy: we will need to collaborate with people who are not like us (using encounter to build productive relationships); we will need to develop our cognitive capacity so that the way we make sense of the world is up to the task. Operating in the blue brain will become increasingly the norm, and the red brain can be discarded for what it is: the shadow of an earlier age.

ACKNOWLEDGEMENTS

The idea for this book has been in my mind since the completion of *The Success Zone* in 2009. In that book, Andrew Mowat, Doug Long and I laid out what we had learned about "two brains" but there were big gaps in our understanding; for example: Where did the red brain come from? Why did it persist? How could you make it disappear? Resolving each of these questions has taken time and it was only when my own red brain faded away in early 2017 that the time was right. However, being so close to this subject for so long – and having my own development so intimately linked to it – I found it hard to find the right approach. I abandoned the manuscript I drafted in 2017 and wrote this one through 2018.

Matt Church, the founder of Thought Leaders, has been a continual support for my endeavours and prompted the change from "red zone" (used in the 2009 book) to "red brain" used in this book. Without his clarity of thinking and amazing ability to see through the unnecessarily complex to the simplicity beyond, this book may never have seen the light of day.

None of the profound changes in my own brain, which helped form the ideas in the book, would have occurred without the experience of coaching more than two hundred senior leaders over the last seven years; too numerous to mention all by name. I thank each of you.

A special mention to Meg Hansen, principal of Westbourne Grammar, and Gerald Bain-King, principal of CBC St Kilda, for the regular conversations over the last two years that helped shape and clarify my ideas.

I am most grateful to my editor, Nicola Dunicliff-Wells, whose advice and suggestions – and, yes, challenges – have proved immensely helpful, making this a much better book.

To my wife, Maryse, thank you for your support, and for helping me in key areas of my development.

Lightning Source UK Ltd.
Milton Keynes UK
UKHW022010100622
404171UK00009B/222